A.C. Marts

THE GENEROSITY
OF AMERICANS:

ITS SOURCE
—
ITS ACHIEVEMENTS

ARNAUD C. MARTS

Foreword by Dr. Norman Vincent Peale

PRENTICE-HALL, INC., ENGLEWOOD CLIFFS, N.J.

Printed in the United States of America

Library of Congress Catalog Card Number: 66-10952

T 35117

Prentice-Hall International, Inc., *London*
Prentice-Hall of Australia, Pty. Ltd., *Sydney*
Prentice-Hall of Canada, Ltd., *Toronto*
Prentice-Hall of India (Private) Ltd., *New Delhi*
Prentice-Hall of Japan, Inc., *Tokyo*

This book is dedicated

to the 40,000,000 Americans who help to make a better world by their generous gifts each year to our forces of religion, education, health, welfare, culture and social justice

and

to the memory of the endless chain of generous men and women in all past generations of Western civilization whose private generosity pioneered the civilizing agencies which benefit all of us and which moved Western man toward his vision of a nobler life for all mankind.

FOREWORD

I have found *The Generosity of Americans: Its Source— Its Achievements,* by Arnaud Marts, to be one of the most completely interesting and profitable books that I have read and enjoyed in my reading experience.

This fascinating work is a fast-moving story which concentrates the reader's attention, as no other book has done, upon a single, extremely important strand in the complex fabric of Western civilization, the strand of man's desire for a nobler world for all mankind. And it explains the means which Western man used across the centuries to pioneer those forces which have moved humanity forward toward that goal.

Indeed this is one of those "only-one-of-its-kind" books which come off the press very rarely. It will fill a too-long-vacant spot on the library shelves which display the numerous histories of Western civilization.

Have you perhaps ever searched the files of a great library for a single volume which would concentrate on the deep and basic urge of Western man to achieve a better world, one which would clearly tell of the practical steps which successive generations have taken over nineteen centuries to make progress toward that goal? If you have searched for such a book which would give you a fast-moving picture of Western man's struggle toward higher levels of freedom and culture, you will understand exactly what I mean by the above-mentioned phrase concerning "a too-long-vacant spot."

This book by Arnaud Marts will occupy that space and in an extraordinarily creative manner. The story has been waiting long to be told, for there *was* (and still is) a continuing and everlasting urge in the hearts and spirits of Western men for a better life for all mankind. Indeed this is a motivation for the history being written today. There were (and still are) men and women in every generation of Western civilization who have never ceased to dream and to struggle toward the goals of refinement, knowledge, human dignity and freedom. The whole drama of this deeply felt need of mankind moves across these pages, portrayed by one who knows this story as do few others; and moreover who tells the story with superb narrative skill.

This book pinpoints the motivating source of the unquenchable urge for a better world. With an acute historical sense it traces clearly and convincingly the irresistible movement of this urge across Europe and America. It describes the basic tool which Western man has used (and still uses) to pioneer and build the major institutions of progress toward civilized refinements.

The profound scholarship of this book is evident in its comprehensive thoroughness, giving as it does the time and place of the creation of these vital refinements of civilization: the cathedral, the school, the hospital, the foundling home, the university, the leprosarium, the pictorial arts, sculpture, music, literature and human freedom.

The basic tool which Western man has used *and still uses* to pioneer and develop the civilized refinements which we now enjoy is *private generosity for the public good*. Ambitious Western man did not wait for remote and benign rulers to give him the better world of which he dreamed; he used his own initiative and money, joined with that of his fellows, to create refinements of life as they were needed. Nor did he create agencies of refinement without plan or leadership. There was one channel and never-failing spiritual motivation for this progress of Western civilization. It was the Christian Church. The Church taught successive generations of Western men the ideal of charity and benevolence and the practice of private generosity. Actually the Church often acted as "fiscal agent" for the generosity of its members, using their gifts to establish the first schools, hospitals, universities and welfare agencies; and, in fact, to introduce the arts of architecture, painting, sculpture, music and literature.

So this is not a textbook of theory or philosophy. It is an absorbing story of great events and personalities, with names and dates and places by which we can visualize the shining strand of history as it moves across Europe, the British Isles and the United States. It sparkles with incidents and personalities of many eras but is fully contemporary with America in 1965.

It gives us glimpses of Nero; St. Peter; St. Paul; St. Augustine; Constantine, the Great; Alaric, Gothic conqueror of Rome; St. Patrick; Chaucer; Michelangelo; Bach; Queen Elizabeth I; the generous English merchants who saved England from collapse; Benjamin Franklin; John D. Rockefeller; Winston Churchill, and a hundred others who were active participants in this fascinating story.

The nineteen-century-old practice of private generosity for the public good has reached its highest volume here in America in 1965. Turn the pages to learn of the unbelievable total which this private generosity of Americans will reach this year.

I must add a few words about the author. I have said this book is unique, an "only-one-of-its-kind," a classic in its field. And it is written by a rare and unique person, an "only-one-of-his-kind." One of the outstanding leaders of American philanthropy expressed it very well when he said: "I am quite certain that no similar book exists for no one but Arnaud Marts *could* write a book of this character. His personal contribution to the well-being of mankind is almost monumental."

I have cherished the friendship of Dr. Marts for over a quarter of a century and know very well indeed the outstanding quality of his mind and heart. I consider him one of the truly wisest men I have ever known. No man in history has done more than he to bring to its great heights the noble strand of private generosity for the public good.

To him goes the honor of stimulating this profound motivation more than any other one man in America. And, since private giving reached its apex in the United States, Arnaud Marts, therefore, occupies a position in this field that is unparalleled in the entire world. I can say what in his own lovable humility he would never think of articulating, that he is one of the greatest motivators of that shining strand of the history of the Western world which he so movingly describes in this great book.

Norman Vincent Peale

ACKNOWLEDGMENTS

S pecial acknowledgment and thanks are given to Union Theological Seminary of New York for permitting me to withdraw several books on the history of the early Christian era which are not readily available elsewhere.

I am very grateful to Dr. Norman Vincent Peale, distinguished author, columnist, lecturer, radio and TV speaker and minister of Marble Collegiate Church, New York, for the gracious foreword which he wrote for this book. His willingness to take the time in his crowded program to read the manuscript and to write his interpretation and appraisal of my theme and narrative was a great encouragement to me. I am deeply appreciative of his kindness and his help.

My associates in Marts & Lundy, Incorporated, have been very helpful to me, and I thank them for their support—especially Mr. Austin V. McClain, our president. My thanks go also to my secretary, Mrs. Edelman, and to the manager of our western office, Mrs. Walker, for their long hours of work involved in transposing my penmanship to the typewriter.

I acknowledge with gratitude the encouragement and help given me by my friend, Mr. Hugh Moore, a successful businessman and himself an exemplar of the spirit of generosity with which this book deals.

Dr. and Mrs. Paul C. Carter have been of great help to me in the preparation of this book for the publisher. They have read carefully and edited every page and have made many constructive suggestions also. I am very grateful to both of them.

The careful editing of my manuscript by the Reverend Dr. Richard Peterman was very helpful and I am grateful to him.

Finally, I acknowledge with gratitude the encouragement of my wife, Anne, whose interest held me for over two years to the laborious task of digging into scores of volumes for the facts which were needed for the narration of the story of generosity over the long reaches of time and space.

ARNAUD MARTS

CONTENTS

I

THE BACKGROUND AND

THE PURPOSE OF THIS BOOK

A unique and astonishing phenomenon of life in the United States is the seemingly unlimited generosity of money, time and energy which millions of our private citizens give each year in voluntary efforts to create a better life for their neighbors and for their communities. Wherever, in communities small and large, there is suffering or injustice, or wherever a social problem is exposed to public knowledge, or wherever greater educational facilities are needed a group of responsive and generous citizens will always respond and undertake to help.

Such responsiveness has led to:

1) over 975,000 private service and cultural agencies, manned and financed by private generosity for the public good.

2) 30,000,000 private citizens serving as volunteer workers and officers of these agencies without compensation.

3) 40,000,000 private citizens making voluntary annual gifts to support these private agencies in their efforts to create a better America.

4) private generosity of the American people which will reach the unprecedented total of $11 billion in 1965.

Of course, these same generous Americans also pay immensely larger sums through taxation for the welfare, educational and health programs of our local, state and federal governments.

THE EXTENT OF AMERICAN PHILANTHROPY

This vast expanse of voluntary and privately financed service for the public good makes up what is called "American Philanthropy." It is a multi-billion-dollar manifestation of the freedom of private citizens in our democracy to take the initiative in meeting community problems.

More than 975,000 units of service deal with four categories of contributors and six categories of agencies, involving the $11 billion of American generosity each year.

These more than 975,000 private agencies include thousands of our colleges and schools; thousands of our hospitals, orphanages and old folks homes; hundreds of thousands of our churches of all faiths; practically all of our youth agencies, such as Boy Scouts, Girl Scouts, Y.M.C.A. and Y.W.C.A.'s. Y.M.H.A. and Y.W.H.A.'s, C.Y.O.'s and many other character-building agencies; all of our Red Cross Chapters; forty organized campaigns against diseases such as cancer, heart, infantile paralysis, tuberculosis and many other health organizations and their local branches; thousands of public institutions, such as libraries, museums, art galleries and zoos.

Our people give just about one-half of this vast generosity —$5 billion—to our churches and other religious movements of all faiths. We give 17 percent of it to our educational institutions and agencies, about 12 percent to our hospitals and health agencies, about 15 percent to welfare agencies and the balance to a variety of other agencies.

AN EXCHANGE OF HYPOTHETICAL MEMOS

These two hypothetical memos (with authentic figures) will underscore the almost unbelievable dimensions of present-day American private generosity for the public good:

MEMO

To: The 30,000,000 Volunteer Workers and Officers of the 975,000 Independent, Non-governmental Agencies of Education, Health, Religion, Youth Guidance, Welfare, Relief, Art, Culture, Community and Social Betterment.

Everywhere,

United States of America.

December 31, 1964

Herewith is this year's final installment of our annual gifts to you for the support of the voluntary service you are rendering to our beloved America.

This brings the total of our gifts to you in 1964 to over $10 billion.

We hope and plan to give you a like total or more in 1965. Please keep up your good work.

We thank you for all the time, talent, energy, goodwill, money and dedication you are putting into your voluntary services to the people of America.

Gratefully yours,

40,000,000 Voluntary American Contributors

MEMO

To: 40,000,000 Voluntary American Contributors

Everywhere,

United States of America

January 4, 1965

Thank you with all our hearts for the over $10 billion you have given in 1964 to the 975,000 independent agencies of human well-being which we are serving as volunteers.

We know very well that these gifts represent a vast amount of unselfish denial by you of pleasures, comforts and luxuries which you could have purchased for yourselves and your loved ones.

Your expressions of gratitude to us for our expenditure of time, energy and money help to make our own lives brighter and finer.

Thank you again for your support *so generously given.*

Gratefully yours,

30,000,000 Volunteer Workers and Officers of America's Independent Agencies for Public Service.

AMERICAN GENEROSITY IS DURABLE AND PERMANENT

Private generosity for the public good and betterment of man is one of the most durable factors of our national life. It *survived* the social and political and moral upheavals of the past thirty years, contrary to excited prophecies of its impending collapse before the rising tides of federal taxation and spending. Year by year it has grown larger in volume and more creative in purpose.

In 1964 private generosity for the public good reached the highest total volume in the history of America, and in the history of any other nation on Earth.

This growth in annual generosity was a surprise to many prophets of recent years. These negative prophets have been "parroted" by hundreds of other citizens who spoke without full understanding of the depth and potency of the American's urge to "lend a hand" in creating a finer world.

The first prophecy was that of a well-meaning businessman deeply disturbed by President Franklin D. Roosevelt's New Deal. He purchased a full page in a leading newspaper of a great city and inserted an advertisement entitled "Don't Kill the Goose that Lays the Golden Eggs." It was directed to heads of colleges, hospitals, youth agencies, Red Cross and all other institutions supported by private generosity. He warned them to fight against "punitive taxation, governmental extravagance, destruction of ingenuity, and initiative," adding "When the goose is killed, it stops laying golden eggs." He concluded his ad with a prophecy of dire consequences: ". . . let me tell you that you are on your last round-up. The future solicitor will be compelled to make his appeal for dollars and dimes contributions."

The fallacy of this one man's prophecy is revealed by the following gifts and bequests—all made after the ad appeared:

$87 million from Mrs. Mathew Astor Wilks, daughter of Hetty Green, to sixty-three philanthropic institutions.

$60 million from Mr. & Mrs. Milton Hershey of Pennsylvania to the Hershey Industries Institution.

$33 million from the Callaway Mills of La Grange, Georgia, to the Callaway Community Foundation.

$50 million from the four children of the late Joseph N. Pew to the Pew Memorial Foundation.

$40 million from Eugene Higgins to four universities.

$50 million from Julius Rippel of Newark to the Fanny E. Rippel Foundation.

$30 million from George R. White of Boston to hospitals and other philanthropies.

$10 million from Clyde H. Harris of Oregon to the Seventh-day Adventist Church.

The other prophecy was uttered about 1934 by the distinguished president of one of our great universities:

> In the history of the University we have arrived at the end of an era during which most generous and great gifts were received from many different individuals for the endowment of the work of the University. . . . The great fortunes and the large accumulations which made these benefactions possible are either dissipated or destroyed . . .
> . . . . Should these great fortunes be renewed, either in

whole or in part, an extravagant government stands ready to take a great portion of their annual income in taxation. . . . A steady flow of gifts from the alumni, moderate in amount but large in number, must be one of the University's chief sources of dependence for its continued usefulness in the years that lie just ahead of us.

Six months later the gifts to the University in the interim were made public. They totaled $655,459—rather a neat sum for six months of a year in the depressed thirties. Had this come in the "steady flow from the alumni, moderate in amount but large in number"? On the contrary, $400,000 had come from one generous man and $245,000 had come in large individual amounts from a relatively few wealthy persons and foundations. Only $9,550.67 had come from the "steady flow."

Since that time, private generosity has continued to surge upward and many gifts and bequests have been made which rank very high on the all-time honor roll of American generosity.

In 1963 gifts and bequests of $1 million (or more) each were made by 178 Americans! The generosity of this small number of persons added up to a total of $662,804,000! The goose has not died; she lays more and larger golden eggs!

THE PERSISTENT GROWTH OF AMERICAN GENEROSITY

During the past dozen years careful records of American generosity have been assembled annually and tabulated by the American Association of Fund-Raising Counsel. These tabulations show that the annual volume of private generosity has advanced steadily from 1954 to 1964—doubled, in fact, in the ten-year period.

Prior to the entry of the AAFRC into this statistical role, very dependable estimates of private generosity were made and published by the Russell Sage Foundation under the direction of F. Emerson Andrews who was then the Director of Research of that Foundation and is now Director of The Foundation Library Center. Estimates, covering the years 1929 to 1949, are to be found in Andrews' volume, *Philanthropic Giving*, published by the Russell Sage Foundation.

The late Robert R. Doane, author of *The Measurement of American Wealth*[1] and *The World Balance Sheet*[2] provided the author with additional data. I have used these several sources on which to base the preparation of the following table of estimates of the volume of private generosity beginning in 1910:

Estimated Annual Totals of Private Generosity, 1910 to 1965:

Year	Total
1910	$ 536 million
1920	$ 750 million
1930	$ 1.2 billion
1940	$ 1.7 billion
1950	$ 4. billion
1954	$ 5. billion
1955	$ 6. billion
1956	$ 6.5 billion
1957	$ 6.7 billion
1958	$ 7.1 billion
1959	$ 7.8 billion
1960	$ 8.2 billion
1961	$ 8.7 billion
1962	$ 9.3 billion
1963	$10. billion
1964	$10.6 billion
1965	$11. billion (est)

The American people during the period 1910-1964, have given an estimated total of $170 billion for our private institutions for the public good. That is a breathtaking sum, but even this vast generosity has not yet succeeded in making America as fine a place for all its citizens as we long to see it

---

[1] (New York and London: Harper & Brothers, Publishers, 1933)
[2] (New York: Harper & Brothers, Publishers, 1957)

become. Social and cultural goals challenge American generosity to still greater efforts and the annual response to the challenge continues to grow.

It will probably reach a total of $11 billion in 1965.

Unique in Our Modern World

There is no other nation in our modern world which matches the United States in our private generosity for public purposes; or in the initiative which our private citizens take in solving community problems.

The runners-up are the English-speaking, self-governing parliamentary nations of the British Commonwealth, notably Canada, Great Britain, Australia, New Zealand and Bermuda. For example England's private generosity in the Tudor era of the sixteenth century saved that nation from social dissolution and, in the words of historian William K. Jordan,[3] "formed the shape of the modern world."

Private generosity is still an honored and respected member of the present-day social forces in the nations of the British Commonwealth, though it is practiced there with more restraint than in the United States.

What about the practice of private generosity for the public good in other nations? In Continental Europe, Asia, Africa, Latin America?

In Modern Europe

The continent of Europe boasts majestic reminders of private generosity of past generations of Western man. They include Western civilization's first universities, schools, hospitals, art museums, cathedrals, monasteries, orphanages—the results of those creative generations, when Rome was termed the "Mother of Charities."

Does private generosity for public purposes still prosper in Continental Europe? Scarcely at all. It is quite forgotten in

---

[3] *Philanthropy in England, 1480-1660* (New York: Russell Sage Foundation, 1959).

most European nations, and even prohibited in those under communistic rule.

The rise of nationalism and the fragmentation of medieval Europe into competitive nations, according to H. G. Wells[4] "has played and continues to play an intensely mischievous part in the world."

It surely "played the mischief" with private philanthropy for the public good as the new nations of the fifteenth century and subsequent centuries took over all the religious, social, educational, welfare and cultural agencies of their peoples, and proceeded to support them with tax receipts and to manage them politically. Thus, when the writer was invited to visit an ancient university in Europe and to advise how funds might be obtained to restore the war-damaged great hall, I mentioned to the officer in authority how the leaders in a comparable city in the United States would create a committee to raise the funds from local citizens to restore their university. He blanched with trepidation, and begged me not to say a word about it in public, saying, "It would offend our national Secretary of Education and might lead him to cut off our support from the national government."

In Latin America

There is very little understanding in the Latin American countries of private generosity for public purposes, and sparse evidence of the use of this social instrumentality. When a man of considerable importance in the business and social and political life of a Latin American nation was asked how much was expected of him in the practice of private philanthropy, he shrugged and said, "A few collections in the street and among businessmen for the poor and, of course, always the offerings in the Church for the poor and the clergy." When asked further if there were no schools or hospitals maintained by private generosity, he said, "Oh, yes, but they are the work

---

[4] *The Outline of History* (New York: The Macmillan Company, 1921), II, p. 431.

of the Christian missionaries and the Roman Catholic orders, and they bring money with them." The Latin American governments give no encouragement to generous donors by way of tax concessions.

Asia and Africa

There is scarcely an Asian or an African nation in which there is not an "American University" or an "American School" or an "American Hospital," and in which there are not also hospitals, orphanages, or schools, bearing the names of orders of Roman Catholic missioners.

The fruits of generosity are there to be seen and used, but they are the fruits of the generosity of mission societies from America and from other Christians of other nations.

DE TOCQUEVILLE'S COMMENTS ON AMERICAN GENEROSITY[5]

The distinguished French traveler and diarist, Alexis de Tocqueville, observed the uniqueness of the American habit of private generosity for the public good over 125 years ago. After his first visit to America, he wrote philosophically and delightfully about the American scene.

De Tocqueville was astonished by our willingness to give generously of our private means for social improvements; it was apparently a new experience for him. He exclaimed to his diary that when Americans see the need for a school or hospital or a church or some other cultural service, a few local citizens form an association (or a committee) to meet that need, provide the leadership, then support it.

It is the individual (or several individuals in voluntary association) who attempt social improvements—not the government, he noted. He observed that in France the government would initiate such a movement, and in England a gentleman of rank would take the lead.

He asked his diary if this practice of the plain citizens of

---

[5] Cf. *The Happy Republic: A Reader in de Tocqueville's America,* George E. Probst, ed. (New York: Harper & Brothers, Publishers, 1962).

America was just a matter of impulse or chance, or did it reveal some inherent relationship between democratic equality and the voluntary association of citizens for the public welfare. A thoughtful question to be dealt with later.

HOW AND WHY DID THIS VAST GENEROSITY DEVELOP IN AMERICA? AND NOWHERE ELSE?

These questions are intriguing, but no one has been able to give me documented answers. Generous men have been asked why this practice is unique in America. Their answer: "I didn't know it was. Don't all civilized people give like we do?" The questions have been asked of students and teachers of history, sociology and philosophy. They had "never thought of it."

Libraries have been consulted in the belief that our private gifts of $170 billion in the twentieth century for the public good must have attracted the attention of responsible historians and authors. No titles are to be found which trace this cultural force back to its origin. This was particularly disappointing to one who has had a most wholesome respect for historians. No one, evidently, has been especially fascinated by this analytical history; no one has spotlighted it within the larger framework of historical events.

Many analytical histories have traced other single strands in the fabric of the nineteen centuries of Western civilization, in books or magazines or journals. For example: *Rats, Lice and History, The Influence of Naval Power Upon History, The Wheel and Civilization*.

However, no comparable—nor satisfactory—analytical history of generosity or philanthropy or charity is available about the historical origins of this powerful agency for the culture, goodwill and civilized well-being of Western man. There is a very full and detailed history of philanthropy in England from 1480 to 1660[6] by W. K. Jordan, professor of history at Harvard:

---

[6] Jordan, *op. cit.*

but it, of course, is limited to one segment and period of Western civilization.

The haunting question led, over the years, to an accumulated file of clippings, references, pamphlets, comments and personal experiences, leading to a personal resolution: Some day I will track down a fair and honest answer to the question.

Surely, the first white settlers in Massachusetts, New York, New Jersey, Delaware, Pennsylvania, Maryland, Virginia, Carolina and Georgia did not find this spirit of private philanthropy as an indigenous product of the seventeenth century forests and fields—like the tobacco, corn and wild turkeys. No, it was not here before the white man's arrival—nor did he invent it after he arrived.

II

THE SEARCH FOR THE ORIGIN

OF AMERICAN GENEROSITY

B eginning with the assumption that American private
generosity and philanthropy was an *import* rather
than an indigenous product of our Western continent, it is
necessary to backtrack toward the East in search of its source.
The trek must go back from "today" to "yesterday" and then
from "yesterday" a continued backtrack still further eastward
on whatever trail the search might take until, hopefully, the
originating source and motivation of this powerful agency of
civilization and culture might be found.

THE EASTWARD TRAIL—TO ENGLAND

This backtrack search for the historic origins of this import to America—of private generosity for the public good—
stopped first in England because our first settlers came from
there. It was during the Tudor period of social emergency that
the early settlers from England came to America. They and
their parents had lived through the years during which the
generosity of English merchants and bankers had saved England from social dissolution. Upon arrival in America they
began immediately to follow that pattern, building churches,
schools and colleges with their own money.

Peter Minuit and his Dutch Reformed religious refugees from the Netherlands arrived in New York at about the same time. They, too, built their churches and schools with their own money. The First Church of Boston, Roxbury Latin School, Harvard University in New England, Marble Collegiate Church and Collegiate School in New York were established by these two groups of settlers in the earliest years. Clearly, American generosity was an import from England, with a strong assist from the Netherlands.

Did England invent private generosity for the public good? Does the search for the originating source of this powerful tool of Western man end in England? By no means! Though the English people have made masterful use of it, it is evident that the spirit and practice of private generosity is older than the English crown itself. It is quite clear that this civilizing force has been a major factor in creating many of England's noblest institutions. So, private generosity for the public good was an *import* into Great Britain just as it was an import into America.

ENGLAND TO ROME

Imported from where? It is not difficult to locate that trail. The direction signs are up all over England, Ireland, Scotland and Wales. They all point eastward to Rome. Prior to the reign of Henry VIII the schools, universities, cathedrals, abbeys, hospitals, foundling homes and relief agencies were all created by Roman Catholic charity. The Christian Church was the main conduit which brought these civilizing forces to Great Britain. The great teachers of Great Britain were Christian teachers: King Alfred the Great, translator of the New Testament into early English; the Venerable Bede; St. Patrick; the Augustinian Fathers; Alcuin and so on. Clearly, the institutions and the spirit of generosity had been brought to England via the conduits of the Roman Catholic Church from the capitol city of the Roman Catholic Church, Rome.

From Rome Farther Eastward

The originating source of the spirit and practice of private generosity for the public good is not found at Vatican City. Rome was the most important transmission station in the power network, but not the generating *source* of this potent civilizing power. The trail backtracks still farther.

Again, the direction signs at Rome are everywhere, and all continue to point toward the East. The trail is well known. It is the trail which Peter and Paul and other apostles of Jesus Christ took westward from Palestine with the "good news" of the Kingdom of Heaven. The trek moves through Macedonia, Greece, Athens, Philippi, Antioch and Galilee to Jerusalem, where the motivating source of American private generosity for the public good is to be found.

The Birth of Western Civilization—27 b. c.

The Roman Empire arose in 27 b. c. when Augustus Caesar became its first emperor, following the assassination of Julius Caesar and the fall of the Republic of Rome. Augustus ruled from 27 b. c. to 14 a. d., establishing the Roman Empire for the next 400 years.

Historians accept the reign of Augustus as the starting point of Western civilization. Such a date does not overlook or underrate the vast contributions made previously to the civilizing and cultural development of man and which carried over, even until the present, into the culture of Western man. Greece, Israel, Egypt, and Persia had passed on to mankind enormous cultural, spiritual, artistic, philosophical and intellectual values —all were priceless possessions of the new, young Western world. These older values were rich assets as youthful Western man began in the first century to create new patterns of community life which were to become known as Western civilization.

Rome was the first in the thousand-year series of world-dominating empires to face westward in its major efforts to conquer, to rule, to prosper. Other great empires which preceded Rome—Egypt, Persia, Phoenicia, Greece—had faced to the East. They had never really penetrated the vast area which is now western Europe, Great Britain, northern Europe, except for the relatively narrow littoral north shores of the Mediterranean which could be reached readily by ship.

Pity poor, young Alexander the Great of Macedon, for instance, for his ignorance of the West. He conquered his whole world eastward, clear into the heart of faraway India, including Greece, Asia Minor, Syria, Egypt, Parthia, Iran and Persia.

When Alexander died at Babylon in 323 B. C. at the age of thirty-three, sighing, "There are no more worlds to be conquered," he was facing in the wrong direction, never knowing that at his back, toward the setting sun, lay resources beyond the dreams of man.

THE ROMAN EMPIRE EXPANDED WESTWARD

The Roman Empire knew very well the value of the West. Julius Caesar had seen much of western Europe and of Britain in his campaigns. His accounts of these campaigns in Latin have sharpened the brains of millions of American high school boys and girls—"All Gaul is divided into three parts."

The early Roman emperors promptly turned their attention to the West. Caligula and Claudius, third and fourth emperors, probably went personally with the Roman army as far as Britain in the first century (37 A. D.-47 A. D.). Also in the first century, Emperors Galba, Vitellius and Vespasian made journeys of conquest to Germany, France or Britain. Emperor Trajan, about 100 A. D., built the famous Trajan Wall in England, remnants of which are still to be seen.

This imperial interest in western Europe and Britain resulted in the construction of roads, fortifications, and cities, in the West. All of them served to prepare the commerce, settlements and civic framework for Western civilization.

THE MOTIVATING SOURCE OF GENEROSITY (30 A. D.)

Having established the starting point of Western civilization, and having identified the Roman Empire as the temporal power which was to construct the political and civic framework for Western civilization, it becomes necessary to identify the motivating source of the spiritual power which would refine and enrich the life of Western man.

It is found in Palestine, near the eastern shore of the Mediterranean Sea, the *Mare Nostrum* of the mighty Roman Empire. It was in the year 30 A. D., just sixteen years after Augustus Caesar, the first emperor of the Roman Empire died.

This was the year in which Jesus of Nazareth died on a cross on a hillside just outside the walls of Jerusalem. It was at this time and place that Jesus launched his vision of the Kingdom of Heaven on Earth.

This teaching of Jesus about a Kingdom of Heaven on Earth, in which men will act toward each other in love, seems like a very simple lesson accepted readily in theory and neglected rather diligently in practice. Why did it explode into a revolutionary force that literally changed the history of Western civilization?

It came at a time when men's hearts were hungry for new spiritual stimuli, and their response to it was astonishingly enthusiastic. Multitudes followed Jesus to hear him speak his simple words. Thousands crowded around him. Many pressed closer to see and touch him at the Sea of Galilee where he was obliged to get into a small boat and speak to them from water too deep for them to wade through to him.

And on the green slope, where he preached, 5,000 men—plus a like number of women and children—swarmed around him and stayed on and on without lunch or supper.

The Roman and Jewish worlds were ripe for such a "new deal." The little nation of Judaea was thoroughly unhappy and distressed, after many bitter and exasperating experiences.

The Hebrews felt that something was very wrong and they knew something different was needed to set it right.

The Roman world was in even worse spirits. The first two centuries of their empire were years of peace and great material prosperity, but they were also years of moral, spiritual and political disintegration. The rulers and the wealthy families of Rome had all the luxuries the world could produce anywhere. Their ships and traders roamed the known world for treasures for the wealthy of Rome, paying prices that astonished, even disgusted, the barbarians.

But knowledge, science, work and enterprise were ignored or left to slaves or left to hired professionals. The result was widespread unhappiness and corruption. The common people were disgusted with their rulers and without hope for their own lives. Thus, when the barbarians invaded, the citizens offered no resistance. Indeed, some of them even joined the invaders. Obviously, they thought there was nothing left worth fighting for.

It was into such a world that this young man, Jesus, held out the power of a kingdom of brotherly love which could change the world. It was the "good news," the Gospel. It dealt with that sort of a possible new world which Jesus' disciples were soon to carry to all parts of the Roman world. It was on the cornerstone of "love for thy neighbor" that the Christian Church was soon to rise.

LOVE FOR GOD AND MAN

On a spring evening in 30 A. D., Jesus gathered His twelve disciples for a final supper, just before His crucifixion on the following day. It was to be one of His last opportunities to teach them His message—a message to the world. He summed up the essence of the Gospel in a few sentences. He wasted no words nor time. Twice He gave them this command: "A new commandment I give unto you, that ye love one another; even as I have loved you, that ye also love one another. By this shall

all men know that ye are my disciples, if ye have love one to another."

The command which Jesus had given them—"to love thy neighbor as thyself"—was the central precept which they passed on to all their young church groups. Every epistle in the New Testament underscores this command.

Paul's lyrical praise of charity in his epistle to the little church at Corinth, Greece, has become part of the literature of Western civilization. Countless boys and girls through the centuries have recited those beautiful words in the King James version: "Now abideth faith, hope, charity, these three; but the greatest of these is charity."

Paul used the Greek word *caritas* for charity, a word meaning love, but not love for the members of one's own family. (The Greeks have a word for that love, too.) But *caritas* is the Greek word for a much wider love—the love for mankind, as a whole. In other words, it is the brotherhood of man, concern for all mankind.

This was the nature of the love Jesus taught His disciples. This was the love they in turn taught thousands of persons whom they drew into the Christian Churches they gathered together. This was the love which the Church carried along the path of Western civilization.

Paul put the message in different words in his letter to the Church of Collosus. As translated by J. B. Phillips, he said to them: "And above everything else, be truly loving for love (*caritas*) is the golden chain of all virtues." John, the Elder, who wrote three epistles of instructions about 100 years later, interpreted Jesus' central "good news" in these three words: "God is love."

THE TWO MAJOR CONDUITS OF WESTERN CIVILIZATION

The two most powerful forces in the shaping of all Western civilization were the Roman crown and the Christian religion. They were born within a short span of a half century; each moved westward, but in bitter hostility to each other during their first four centuries.

Edward Gibbon observed the interactions upon each other of these two forces: the quiet penetration of the humble religion into the hearts and minds of man and the final erection of "the triumphant banner of the cross on the ruins of the Capital." [1]

Western civilization was brought by these two conduits across the early centuries of Western man. The Roman Empire was the conduit of the political skills and the military power; the Christian Church was the conduit for the spiritual, intellectual and cultural elements of Western man.

High among these latter values was the spirit and practice of private generosity for the public good, which the Christian Church called "charity."

---

[1] *Decline and Fall of the Roman Empire*, D. M. Low, ed. (New York: Washington Square Press, Inc., 1962), I, Chapter 15, p. 181.

III

EVIDENCES OF THE SPIRIT

AND PRACTICE OF GENEROSITY

ACROSS WESTERN CIVILIZATION

Having located the motivating source of private generosity for the public good of Western man, the historical spotlight must search the vast geographical and historical expanse of Western civilization for evidences of its spirit and practice during the past nineteen centuries.

These evidences and achievements of generosity will be found in instances of the voluntary generous acts of individuals or groups:

1. to provide food and shelter for the needy poor who are not part of the giver's own family;
2. to build a church or place of worship;
3. to build or maintain a non-profit hospital, or leprosarium, or nursing home for the sick and suffering;
4. to build or maintain a foundling home for homeless children;
5. to build or maintain a home for the aged or infirm or neglected;
6. to provide care for the blind or otherwise handicapped;
7. to build or maintain a school for children;

8. to create or maintain colleges and universities for youth;
9. to support character-building agencies for adolescents;
10. to mount a community movement against an injustice or a disease or some other social evil;
11. to encourage and aid the development of literature and the arts—architecture, painting, sculpture, music;
12. to defend and promote human freedom, and the rights and dignity of the individual.

Such unselfish acts of private generosity for the benefit of other persons mark the trail of one of the noblest instincts of Western man and lead to a partial explanation of why 40,000,-000 people of the United States in 1965 are generously giving over $11 billion to private non-profit agencies, to better the life of all our people.

Definitions

A proper orientation requires a brief sketch of the accepted definitions of the key words: civilization—generosity—charity —philanthropy, from *Webster's Third International Dictionary*:

Civilization—an ideal state of human culture characterized by complete absence of barbarism and nonrational behavior. . . . (The word is derived from the Latin root civis [city]; and thus suggests the adjustment of an individual within the framework of a populated community, as distinct from early man's solitary life in a remote forest or field.)

Generosity—liberality in spirit or act. (Latin root generus; nobility of birth or breeding)

Charity—the act of loving . . . all men as brothers because they are the sons of God. . . . The kindly and sympathetic disposition to aid the needy or suffering. . . . (The word is derived from the Greek root *caritas*.)

Philanthropy—goodwill toward one's fellowmen, especially as

expressed through active efforts to promote human welfare. (The word is derived from two Greek roots: *philo* [love] and *anthropos* [mankind].)

LOVE AND CHARITY

Students of the early Christian Church unite, almost without exception, in agreeing that the message of the Church was that of *love* and *charity*. The literature of the first three centuries of the Church is full of passages which enjoin love and charity, and which give instances and data concerning the nature and scope of the charity of certain churches. Bishop Chrysostom, for illustration, reported that the charity of the Christian Church in the city of Antioch was supporting 3,000 widows, virgins, orphans, sick, blind and other needy persons.

Tertullian, well-known Roman jurist, who was converted to Christianity at middle age, wrote in his Apologia about 200 A. D., "It is our care of the helpless, our practice of loving kindness, that brands us in the eyes of many of our opponents. 'Only look' they say, 'look how they love one another.' (They themselves being given to mutual hatred.) 'Look how they are prepared to die for one another.' (They themselves being readier to kill each other.)"

The *Encyclopaedia Britannica* describes the generous charity of the early Christians in this passage: "A vast activity animated the early Church, to heal the sick, to feed the hungry, to succour the diseased, to rescue the fallen, to visit the prisoners, to forgive the erring, to teach the ignorant. . . . A mighty power impelled men to deny themselves in the service of others, and to find in this service to others their own true life." [1]

A young Roman emperor, Julian, was so impressed by Christian generosity that when he tried to found a new pagan religion, he incorporated a copy of Christian generosity into his pagan observances.

---

[1] *Encyclopaedia Britannica* (1929), V, p. 634.

THE TEN MAJOR OBJECTS OF GENEROSITY

Charity was a primary enthusiasm of the early Christians. The question is: How did the early Christians give expression to their generous impulses? Able students and researchers have accumulated facts and figures which aid in the discovery of an answer to this practical question.

The following is a list of the ten major objects of the generosity of the typical early Christian congregation during the first three centuries of Western civilization:

1. alms in general.
2. the support of teachers and officials of the Church.
3. the support of widows and orphans.
4. the support of the sick, the infirm and the disabled.
5. the care of prisoners and people languishing in the mines (to which prisoners were condemned).
6. the care of poor people needing burial, and of the dead in general.
7. the care of slaves.
8. the care of those visited by great calamities.
9. the churches furnishing work, and insisting upon work.
10. the care of brethren on a journey (hospitality); and of churches in poverty or any peril.

More detailed information on the above ten practices of generosity in the early Church may be found in the work of Dr. Adolph Harnack, late professor of Church History in the University of Berlin.[2]

A vital factor in an overall view of Christian generosity in the midst of a pagan world was the requirement that a charitable gift *should be made in person.* In other words, a gift must be offered in a personal way as an act of compassionate love from one human heart to another.

---

[2] *The Mission and Expansion of Christianity in the First Three Centuries* (New York: Harper & Row, Publishers, 1962).

THE CHRISTIAN'S TREASURE CHEST

Another vital factor was "the Christian's treasure chest," mentioned by Tertullian, whose church at Rome engaged in the practice: "We have our treasure chest. On the monthly collection day, if he likes, each one puts in a small donation, but only if it be his pleasure and only if he is able; there is no compulsion, all is voluntary."

He also chides his pagan friends, "Our compassion spends more in the streets (in charity) than yours does in the temples."

Still another factor was the Christian home. During the first three centuries of Western civilization, there were no charitable institutions such as hospitals, orphanages or homes for the indigent.

The Christians of the fourth century built the first institutions of this character; consequently, during the first three Christian centuries, every Christian house was ready to provide hospitality for strangers; to take in the infants who had been "exposed" (placed in the street by parents who did not want them); to provide shelter and food for the indigent and the suffering. This private generosity by individual Christian families was over and above the family's contributions to the charities of the Church.[3] It gave further expression to their deep desire to extend the hand of Christian helpfulness to needy and worthy persons.

SPECIFIC INSTANCES OF EARLY CHRISTIAN GENEROSITY (30 A. D.-411 A. D.)

The generous charity which was a vital factor in the creation of Western civilization was not a "cloud nine" abstraction or vision. It was a program of action. It was not a passive philosophical ideal; it was a force. It was a basic motivation of the unselfish desire to be helpful to others, to pay the price for a better world of the future, to "love thy neighbor as thyself."

---

[3] See G. Ulhorn, *Christian Charity in the Ancient Church*, trans. by Sophia Taylor (Edinburgh: T & T Clark, 1883).

Christian charity according to W. E. H. Lecky[4] created a spirit and practice of generosity for others that had been totally unknown to the pagan world. For example, the first hospital was founded by a Roman lady—a Christian, Fabiola. The first asylum for lepers, the first Xenedochia (refuges for strangers), were founded by Christians—one of them founded by a wealthy Roman widow, Paula, and her daughter at Jerusalem. Foundling homes for infants; the elevation and protection of slaves; the suppression of barbarous games and spectacles in the stadium—each was an object of Christian charity. Lecky tells of a Christian monk of a little later generation, the charity of whose life was to plant himself with his small boat at a bridgeless swift stream and to ferry the travelers safely across. Altogether, says Lecky, this spirit of Christian generosity, of concern for others promoted human happiness and determined qualities of character, "which have never been paralleled or approached in the pagan world."

---

[4] *History of European Morals* (New York: George Braziller, Inc., 1955), see especially Vol I, Chapter 3; Vol II, Chapters 4 & 5.

IV

THE FOUNDING OF CHURCHES,

THE CONDUIT OF GENEROSITY

During the last days of Jesus' life, He instructed His disciples to carry His Gospel (good news) to all peoples of the world. Several started out very promptly to obey. Wherever they went they made converts and gathered them into a congregation, which would hold a weekly service of prayer, hymns and instruction in the new faith. Jesus' brother James assembled such a congregation in Jerusalem which held its weekly meetings in Mary's home.

Other disciples established churches elsewhere in Palestine. Peter and Paul, the most energetic of the missionaries, struck out for more distant cities—including Antioch, where the name Christian was first used, Caesarea and Asia Minor.

These two apostles, Peter and Paul, thrust the new Christian faith into the very mainstream of Western civilization by establishing churches throughout Greece, Macedonia and Italy—and eventually at Rome itself, the capital of the Roman Empire, which cost them their lives.

As part of the spiritual instruction in the Christian faith at the weekly meetings, certain virtues were taught and accepted as rudimentary Christian virtues. These virtues were those mentioned by Jesus, especially in the Beatitudes and in the rest of the Sermon on the Mount. High on the list of these Christian virtues was "generosity" which they termed "charity"; that is, "The act of loving all men as brothers because they are the sons of God; the kindly and sympathetic disposition to aid the needy or suffering."

THE LOCAL CHURCH PROGRAM

Local church programs were varied. A part of the program instructed the members in the virtue and the practice of generosity for others. This instruction centered in collections for the poor at every Sunday meeting, and in the periodical agapae or feasts of love. At these love feasts the Holy Communion was celebrated, using bread and wine, in an act of thanksgiving in remembrance of Jesus' sacrifice. Along with this a generous supper was served, mainly for the benefit of the poor of the community, who were regarded as special representatives of Jesus. In addition, food that was saved by fast days belonged to the poor. Deacons and deaconesses were appointed to collect the charity and to see that the needy and poor benefited from it.

The income of the Church was used for the essential maintenance of the clergy and for the cost of public worship, including the feasts of love. The remainder was looked upon as belonging to the poor and was distributed to them by the deacons and the deaconesses in accordance with the judgment of the clergy.

It should be noted that these funds were used not simply for the poor of the congregation or of their own faith, but to aid the widows and orphans, the sick, the aged and the blind of the *whole community*. The charity funds of the Church were used, also, to aid strangers and to comfort prisoners and captives who were treated very severely in the pagan Roman Empire. Smaller struggling congregations were aided regularly and generously by the charity of larger congregations.

JEWISH CHARITY

The major emphasis which the earliest Christians placed upon generosity and charity, was in complete harmony with their earlier religious teachings and practices, for they had been Jews before they became followers of Christ. Jesus was a Jew; so were Peter, Paul, John and James; and all the early Christian apostles were practicing Jews. The followers of the Jewish faith have always been amongst the most generous peoples on Earth. Charity is a basic Hebrew virtue, taught by them and to them, generation after generation. Indeed, the tithe, the giving of 10 percent of income and property to God, is written into the basic law of the Hebrews.

Jesus placed the ancient virtue of generosity high on the list of Christian virtues. His Christian followers of many racial and national strains channeled it enthusiastically into the mainstream of Western civilization, extending it to needy persons of all faiths, or of no faith.

WHY THIS DETAIL ABOUT THESE LITTLE CHURCHES?

This story of the early Christians and of their love and generosity for their fellow men—more than stories of kings, wars, knights—is of prime importance because they were soon to guide and lead the tide of civilization as it swept westward.

These people—unknown men and women—held in their hearts and minds the mustard seed to which their founder had likened His kingdom of heaven.

Their growth was even more spectacular than that of the mustard seed. In 30 A. D., there were perhaps 10,000 believers and followers. By 100 A. D. there were 500,000; by 200 A. D., 2,000,000; by 500 A. D., 15,000,000; by 1000 A. D., 50,000,000; by 1500 A. D., 100,000,000; by 1965, 993,000,000.

By 311 A. D. the little, despised and persecuted Christian Church became the stronger of the two forces which were the major conduits of Western civilization. The Church absorbed the mighty empire and has outlasted it by 1,500 years—and is still vital and growing.

The Church is of far greater significance than the number of its members and its organizational power. It has been of crucial significance in bringing across the centuries, and half the surface of the globe, the spirit of generosity, of concern for our fellows and of the realization that, in the words of H. G. Wells,[1] "voluntary self-abandonment to some greater end, without fee or reward, was an acceptable idea to men, or that anyone propounded it . . ." It is the Church which became the conduit for bringing these essential elements of cultural and of spiritual values into the minds and hearts of Western man.

THE UNIQUE ORGANIZATION OF THE EARLY CHRISTIAN CHURCH

It is not entirely clear who the organizing geniuses were that created the structure of the early Christian Church, but it is quite clear that it was a sturdy and durable organization. It is older than any similar organization in the world. It outlasted the Roman Empire which tried desperately to destroy it. It drew its members from many races so that its only common tie was that of its religious faith.

As the local churches multiplied they began to group into synods which used the geographical lines of the Roman provinces. It soon became a custom or a law that the provincial synod should meet each spring and autumn. The presbyters and bishops would be elected delegates to these synod meetings which were held in the presence of large numbers of church visitors who listened eagerly to the discussion of the issues of faith, organization and discipline. The decrees which were issued after the discussions of the synods were called "canons," and these became laws governing the authority of the churches and the Christian conduct of the members.

---

[1] *Op. cit.,* p. 402.

MANAGEMENT FOR THE EXPANDING CHURCH

It was not enough to create the framework of an organization, however sturdy it proved to be. It was more necessary to provide adequate management. This was done by the gradual enlargement of the territorial responsibility of the bishops. In the earliest apostolic years, Peter or Paul or other of the missionary apostles might designate the leader of a single church which he had founded as the bishop. But as the churches grew in size and number, the title of bishop came to be used for the presiding ecclesiastical officer of a group of churches, which was called a synod.

Soon many of the bishops began to establish administrative headquarters at the principal city within his synod or diocese. This headquarters was called his "see," with the see city often being the capital city of the Roman province.

These see cities became extremely important in the evangelizing and administrative programs of the Church; and they became equally important in the charitable programs of the Church, particularly after the persecutions stopped about 312 A. D. and the Church could hold its head up to public view.

Around the bishop's church in each see there began to cluster, with the passing years, various institutions of charity, mercy, healing, education, art and culture. So extensive were the charitable activities of the see cities, that some of them were dubbed "Heaven on Earth."

Since—as the saying goes—all roads lead to Rome, it was natural that the bishop of the see in Rome would gradually become a bishop of special prestige among other bishops of the early Church, for the city of Rome was dominant in all that went on in the Roman Empire. The first bishop of Rome, according to Eusebius in his *History of the Christian Church*, written in 324 A. D., was St. Peter the apostle. The primacy of the bishops of Rome developed quite steadily, and since the year 190 A. D. the bishop of Rome has been called the "pope." The first to have used that title was Pope Victor—189-199 A. D.

In the twentieth century—a time of organization—it has been concluded that the early Church's organizational structure reveals excellent planning! A sound structure was created which could sustain the administrative load of a rapidly expanding Christian community.

A quick survey of the expansion of the young Church in the first three centuries reveals that an amazing number of congregations were established—to form what we have termed the conduit of charity, generosity and brotherhood which thrust its way westward.

A characteristic of the early Christians was their energy. They were not lazy, either as individuals or as a church group. They treasured the dignity of the individual, and they believed that one important element in an individual's dignity was his willingness to work to support himself and his family. This was a prime Christian virtue which came westward through the conduit to our early culture in America.

Paul believed strongly in the duty of the individual to support himself and was, evidently, criticized by one of the early Churches which he founded in Greece. He took a job in his trade as tentmaker while he was preaching to his little congregation on the Sabbath. They thought he should let them support him and told him so. He disagreed.

Energy and zeal was the spirit of each little church, as well as of individuals. The Christians had some "good news" which they believed would bless the lives of all who would hear it and live by it. They believed it would save and transform their shaky world—they proclaimed their Gospel, "good news" to all whom they could reach, or to all who would listen. Thousands did listen and believed.

In Rome and Italy

Tacitus speaks in his *Annals* (60 A. D.) of the "ingens multitude" of Christians in Rome during Nero's reign. Pope Cornelius reported in a letter to Eusebius (253 A. D.) that there were in Rome forty-six priests and 100 clerics of lower orders, and they were supporting 1,500 needy persons, including orphans and widows.

Churches were also being established at many places in central and southern Italy in the last half of the first century A. D. —at Naples, Ostia, Portus and even in Pompey, the latter being destroyed by the eruption of Vesuvius in 79 A. D.

In northern Italy strong churches were established quite early—at Ravenna in 120 A. D.; Milan, 200 A. D.; Venice, 240 A. D.; Bologna and Brescia, 300 A. D.—and by 300 A. D. there were sixty bishops in Italy outside of Rome.

In southern France, along the seacoast, which was settled by Greek immigrants who sailed around Sicily, the Greek Christians established churches between 100 A. D. and 250 A. D. at Marseilles, Arles, Lyons, Viennes and other points. The churches in this area flourished so promptly that by 314 A. D., sixteen bishops were reported in attendance at the Synod of Arles.

Evidence of the expansion of the churches elsewhere appears in the records of early synod meetings. In 200 A. D. seventy bishops from the coast cities of Roman North Africa attended the Synod of Carthage. In 318 A. D., 100 bishops attended the Synod of Alexandria from Alexandria and Egypt, and from as far away as Thebes and Libya.

It is recorded by Iranaeus that bishops from Cologne, Germany, and from Trier, Belgium, attended the Synod of Arles in 314 A. D. Bishops from England, also, representing the Synods of York, London and Lincoln, were reported in attendance at the Synod of Arles in 314 A. D.

In short, the Church was moving swiftly forward in the first, second and third centuries of the Christian era, and was teaching millions of people in successive generations the civilizing virtues of generosity, brotherhood and love for mankind as a whole.

By 300 A. D., there were 7,000,000 living Christians in the Roman Empire, and the number of churches and members was increasing each year.

Fortunately—at least, for us in America in 1965—the ablest of the early Christian missionary apostles turned their faces toward the West.

Jesus had commanded his disciples to go into all the world and preach his Gospel. Why did Peter and Paul, the most successful of the missionaries, turn westward, instead of eastward or southward? [2] While the question cannot be answered here, it is to be emphasized at this point that these two great missionaries went northward from Jerusalem through Asia Minor, then crossed the Aegean Sea into Greece (now a part of Europe), established churches there and then moved on westward to Rome, with at least one of them reaching Spain.

Because of this westward move, the Christian Church brought its infusion of charity—of love for God and humanity—into the blood stream of Western civilization at the very earliest stages of the latter's own thrust to the West.

EVERY CHURCH AN AGENCY FOR GENEROSITY

Since one of the primary objectives of the early Christian Church was to inculcate and stimulate the practice of generous charity and the love for God and mankind, and since Christians of those early centuries believed deeply in Jesus' command to "Love thy neighbor as thyself," it may be assumed quite fairly that each of the several thousand Christian Churches of the first three centuries of Western civilization was an agency for the teaching and practice of generosity, all of them faithful to charity as a basic Christian virtue.

EACH CHRISTIAN WAS A PRACTITIONER OF GENEROSITY

It may also be assumed that the vast majority of the many millions of Christian people of the first three centuries were sincere practitioners of generous charity.

Competent historians have documented the fact that members of the Christian Churches during the first three centuries

---

[*] See Selected Readings in the Supplement.

were dedicated and responsive to the teachings of their Lord. If this be the case, there were 7,000,000 living practitioners of Christian generosity by 300 A. D., and their number was to be multiplied in the immediate future.

Charity's Blessings Flow Both Ways

This unselfish love, *caritas,* was having a double effect upon Western civilization. First, it was introducing a new spirit in human society, a sense of concern for others. This was a direct blessing to society of that day, and to the peoples of all future generations, including our own in 1965, for it was to develop a tradition of generosity in Western man which would become a very essential part of our culture.

Secondly, it was having another civilizing effect: The practice of generous charity was refining the natures and the spirits of the men and women who were being generous.

The very act of kicking a poor beggar into the gutter degrades the man who does it. Conversely, the very act of holding out a charitable hand to an unfortunate person refines and civilizes the person who does so. Freud has said that each love we experience, each loving act we perform, leaves a deposit— a result—on our own mind and personality.

Is it not true, therefore, that the charity of the early Christians blessed those who received it, and equally refined and blessed those who gave it?

Lowell had Jesus say in *The Vision of Sir Launfal*: "Who gives himself with his alms feeds three, himself, his hungering neighbor, and Me."

V

FALSE CHARITY IN

THE PAGAN ROMAN EMPIRE

(27 B. C.-311 A. D.)

In relating the generosity of the Christians during the first three centuries of Western civilization, the question arises: Was there any comparable generosity for the public good being practiced by all the pagan citizens of the Roman Empire, who far outnumbered Christians and Jews? The answer to that question was summed up in four words by Dr. G. Uhlhorn: "They had *not* charity." [1] A possible exception was the *alimentatione*, free meals for poor children, instituted by a kindly emperor, Nerva, who ruled two years—96-98 A. D. (Some believe this was sparked by the examples of Christian charity in every city.)

Other historians, notably Gibbon and Wells, comment at some length upon the high level of Roman prosperity of that period and the low level of freedom, morality, education and political stability.

A Glittering Substitute for Genuine Generosity

Roman emperors, victorious generals, senators, consuls and political candidates devised ostentatious substitutes for private

---

[1] *Op. cit.*

36

generosity which fooled the populace into the belief that their leaders were most generous to them.

For instance, Augustus, the first emperor, won a reputation as a model benefactor of the Roman people. He, himself, published a long list of grants and gratuities which he had distributed. Time and time again, he distributed money to as many as 250,000 persons in celebration of an anniversary or as a donation to the colonies of his soldiers. Over the years these gifts added up to the equivalent of $30 million. These resources were generated by the booty brought home by his victorious armies and by the taxes laid upon conquered nations. In addition, it was the practice (required) of colonies and cities to make gifts to him on the occasion of his military triumphs. Occasionally he would remit such a gift, which would add to his reputation for benevolence.

A greatly appreciated feature of his generosity was his repeated extravagant expenditure for public spectacles and gladiatorial entertainments, which involved as many as 10,000 contestants. Other emperors and officials also used these public games as demonstrations of their "charity." On one occasion Caesar gave a banquet at which 22,000 tables were set for the populace. Free grain was distributed by many officials to hundreds of thousands of persons. This was called generosity or charity, but it was more truly an investment in political stability, because the Roman leaders knew that revolutions against loss of liberty are promoted by mass hunger.

All of this so-called "charity" or generosity had a demoralizing effect upon pagan Rome. The people became a pleasure-demanding, work-shunning people who cheered each new political leader, for he would surely give them another handout of money or grain, or would stage another stupendous week-long game in the stadium, or would set a great feast of food and wine. They were so corrupted by this false generosity that they even turned out en masse to greet their monster emperor, Nero, after he had assassinated his own mother.

"They knew not charity" nor did they know some of the

other simple virtues of honor, work, truth and love for their fellows. One of the reasons the pagan Romans hated the Christians so vehemently was due to the animosity which the Christians felt and expressed toward the corruption and selfishness of their pagan neighbors, which had been accelerated by the false charity offered by demonic rulers.

VI

THE PERSECUTIONS OF
THE CHRISTIANS
(64 A. D.-312 A. D.)

Beginning in the year 64 A. D., during the reign of Emperor Nero, efforts were made—and continued for the next 200 years—by certain of the emperors and provincial officers and citizens of pagan Rome to harass and persecute the followers of the Christian faith. There were many reasons for a general hostility to the Christians. Perhaps their moral earnestness aroused the dislike of persons whose moral standards were less exacting. Perhaps some Christians assumed displeasing attitudes of moral superiority. Christians severely condemned the cruel games in which gladiators fought with each other and with wild beasts, frequently to the death. And the Christian Church ordered their members not to attend the theater where obscene and immoral acts were frequently performed on the stage for the entertainment of the audience.

The most deadly hatred of the Christians, however, was probably generated by their faithful observance of the commandment "Thou shall have no other gods before me." The emperor of pagan Rome was a god, and as such was to be worshiped by Romans, along with their other gods. The Christians' refusal to worship any of the Roman gods, the emperor included, was a denial of the emperor's divinity and was not to be ignored.

When brought before a magistrate and charged with this disloyalty, a magistrate might offer to dismiss the Christian culprit from the tribunal if he or she would simply cast a few grains of incense upon the altar. If he or she would refuse, a magistrate might have recourse to violence of the scourge or of the rack or of every other act of cruelty to force compliance.

Certain emperors urged leniency, notably Hadrian and Antoninus Pius, while certain other emperors, notably Nero and Decius and Diocletian, encouraged the clamors of the multitude to demand that the accused should be instantly thrown to the lions in a public spectacle.

Gibbon believes that the extent of the persecutions has been greatly exaggerated. Other authorities, notably Eusebius, who lived and wrote in the latter years of the persecutions, give a more dreadful account of the bloody efforts to halt the influence of the growing Christian body.

These persecutions had a surprisingly positive effect upon the vitality of the early Christian Church. They, therefore, gave a comparable impetus to generosity, a major product of the Christian Church.

PERSECUTIONS BY NERO (64 A. D.)

According to Tacitus, Christian baiting began with the burning of Rome in 64 A. D. The cruel—and probably insane— Emperor of Rome, Nero, was accused of responsibility for the famous fire which broke out at Rome on July 8, 64 A. D. in the Circus Maximus and which destroyed two-thirds of the city. Thousands of people lost their lives, and hundreds of thousands of others were rendered homeless and destitute. It was rumored that Nero set the fire in order to be able to show what a beautiful new city he could design—for he fancied himself an architect, as well as an athlete, poet, gladiator and musician.

So fierce were the rumors against him, Nero looked for a scapegoat, and for that role he chose the community of Christians which Peter and Paul and other missionaries of Jesus' Gospel had created.

Tacitus describes the massacre of Christians which follows:

. . . . There was in Rome a race of men . . . commonly called "Crestiani." The name was derived from Chrestus who, in the reign of Tiberius, suffered under Pontius Pilate. By that event the sect of which he was the founder received a blow which for a time checked the growth of a dangerous superstition, but it revived soon after, and spread with recruited vigor not only in Judea—but even in the city of Rome —Nero proceeded with his usual artifice. . . . A number of Christians were convicted, not indeed on clear evidence of having set the city on fire, but rather on account of their sullen hatred of the whole human race.

They were put to death with exquisite cruelty, and to their sufferings Nero added mockery and derision. Some were left to be devoured by dogs, others were nailed to crosses;—many were set on fire to serve as torches. . . . At length the brutality of these measures filled every breast with pity. Humanity relented in favor of the Christians.

PETER AND PAUL WERE VICTIMS

The New Testament does not specifically name the time and place of the deaths of Peter and Paul, but there are many legends to the effect that each of these great apostle missionaries was martyred in Rome in 64 A. D. and the presumption is that they fell in this cruel massacre of Christians by the insane tyrant, Nero.

Legend further goes that Peter was crucified upside down on a cross in order to show further scorn for him, or at his own request to humble himself, and that Paul was beheaded.

DESTRUCTION OF JERUSALEM (70 A. D.)

A few years later another cruel Roman emperor, Vespasian, unleashed a murderous attack upon Jerusalem through his son, General Titus. There had been civil disturbances in the Holy City a few years earlier, when the restoration of the temple had been completed after nearly 100 years of reconstruction, started under Herod the Great.

Suddenly 18,000 men were out of work. King Agrippa was urged to tear part of the temple down and start the rebuilding over again as a make-work project. He refused, but did assent to use temple funds to pave certain streets with marble.

Serious unrest set in among the people. A group of extremists, the Zealots, called the Sicarii, began a series of violent and criminal acts.

Rome ordered a march of 40,000 soldiers against Jerusalem in 66 A. D. from Antioch. They met resistance and were routed in flight. In 67 A. D. another army was mobilized at Ptolemeus, but as the siege of Jerusalem was about to begin in 68 A. D., word came from Rome that Nero had committed suicide. The situation in Rome was as turbulent for the next two years as in Jerusalem. Three men were proclaimed emperor and promptly overthrown, in quick succession. The army made their commander, Vespasian, Roman emperor in 70 A. D.; and he ordered his own son, Titus, to assemble an army at Caesarea and destroy Jerusalem.

Titus succeeded in the task by September, 70 A. D.; Jerusalem was completely leveled, and the Jewish population was destroyed and dispersed with a cruelty which has never been excelled. According to Josephus, over 1,000,000 Jews were slaughtered. It is said that 100,000 were led off to Egypt to slavery, while thousands of others were distributed to Roman amphitheaters to be killed in contests of "sport." Titus presided at two of these celebrations which he held in honor of the birthday of his father, Vespasian, and his brother, Domitian. In these two gala events in the amphitheaters at Caesarea and Beirut, thousands of Jewish captives perished in combats with gladiators and with lions and other wild beasts.

VESPASIAN

But Vespasian went much farther to make sure that the God-loving, zealous Jews could never again challenge the government of Rome. He issued a harsh decree to terminate the Jewish religion for all time. He had already destroyed the temple; he now ordered all outward marks and tokens of the Jews as a separate and distinct people to be erased. He imposed a temple tax of a half shekel upon every Israelite twenty years of age and older, wherever he lived; this tax was to be used for the upkeep of the shrine of the Roman god, Jupiter, on the Capitoline Hill in Rome.

When Titus returned in triumph to Rome, he brought as trophies to his father, the emperor, the treasures and holy vessels of the temple, and certain Jewish dignitaries who were displayed in disgrace in the triumphal procession. Extreme measures were taken by Vespasian to drive the Jews completely out of the Holy City, and to scatter them so widely that they could not again threaten the security of the empire. His cruelty knew no limits.

DECIUS (250 A. D.)

Emperor Decius unleashed an organized persecution of Christians with ferocious cruelty. He tried to destroy completely the Christian Church, murdering thousands of Christians as martyrs. He issued a libellus or certificate to those who would forsake Christianity and return to paganism, the worship of the god-emperor.

In Rome he urged the populace to unspeakable acts of cruelty and public outrage upon the Christians in the spectacles of sport in the amphitheater. Groups of Christians were turned loose in that stadium with hungry wild beasts which tore them to pieces to the cheers of the spectators.

Others were thrown on a burning pyre or roasted to death at a slow fire. Pope Cornelius was one who was martyred by Decius, as were also the bishops of Jerusalem and of Antioch.

VALERIAN AND DIOCLETIAN

Persecutions were begun again by Emperor Valerian in 258 A. D. Among many others Cyprian, Bishop of Carthage, was one of his victims.

Diocletian became emperor in 285 A. D., and within a few years he started a new series of persecutions with a veritable frenzy. During these persecutions many Egyptian Christians had withdrawn to the desert where they lived as hermits. Others followed and soon formed themselves into religious communities. From this start arose Christian monasteries for men.

END OF PERSECUTIONS

Constantine the Great made himself the Emperor of the Roman Empire in 311 A. D. Constantine promulgated an edict of toleration of Christians in 312 A. D.—and mass persecutions were ended. The Church had tottered, but it had survived.

Christians had lost thousands of their number through these cruel mass murders, but they had gained a new strength, a new self-confidence and a new respect from the world of that day— even down to our day—for their supreme courage and cool acceptance of martyrdom for their convictions.

Some of the most precious traditions in the Christian faith —handed down from generation to generation across the centuries—have come about because of these martyrs. For example, Chaucer, the first of England's great poets, celebrated the martyrdom of Cecelia Metellus, a Christian lady of a noble Roman family, in one of his famous *Canterbury Tales.* This story had been told and retold orally from the time of her martyrdom in 225 A. D., and survived to appear 1,200 years later in earliest English literature.

Cecelia was a devout, generous and beautiful Christian lady —a member of the noble Metellus family of Rome. She was a lover of music and sponsored vocal and instrumental music in the services and culture of the early Christian Church. Raphael, one of the most popular painters of all time, painted Cecelia in one of his famous portraits. She is called, "The Saint of Music and the Blind."

In Chaucer's poem, Almachius ordered Cecelia to worship an idol of stone or suffer death. She refused with this reply:

. . . you seek to glorify,
A senseless piece of stone that you would call
A God! Put out your hand and let it fall
Upon it, touch it, taste it! You will find
Your hand says "Stone!" Although your eyes are blind.
People will laugh at you to hear such stuff
As you have uttered, they will think you mad,
For it is known, and commonly enough,
That God Almighty is in Heaven, clad
In glory, and these idols—if you had
The eyes to see it—offer no delight
To you or to themselves; not worth a mite.

Cecelia was tortured for three days.

But all the Christian folk, or such as were
About her then, bound her with sheets to stay
The flow of blood, and she, to the third day,
Lingered in pain yet never ceased in teaching
The faith she fostered, and continued preaching.

Chaucer concludes his tale by relating that she was secretly
buried by Pope Urban, and the Church of St. Cecelia was
erected over her grave. It is still there, a reminder of a noble
Christian lady. Chaucer concludes:

St. Urban and his deacons secretly
Fetched forth her body and buried it by night
Among his saints. Her mansion came to be
The Church of St. Cecelia, hers by right;
St. Urban hallowed it, as well he might.
And in that Church in every noble way
Christ and his saint are honoured to this day.

Bishop Polycarp was another martyr whose brave death
strengthened the spirit of the early Christians. He was the
Bishop of Smyrna, one of the last of the line of "Apostolic

Fathers." Upon his return to Smyrna in 155 A. D.—after a visit to Rome—he found that a great sport festival was in progress, in which several Christians had been put to death in the games. Polycarp was seized, brought into the arena and promised his freedom if he would "revile Christ." He refused. Timber and fagots were prepared; Polycarp was placed upon the pyre; with dignity and unflinching courage he met his death.

St. Ignatius, Bishop of Antioch, was arrested in 110 A. D., condemned to death and taken to Rome to fight the beasts in the amphitheater. On his way he wrote his final epistle to his church in which he said, "Let me be given to the wild beasts, for through them I can attain unto God."

Blandine, according to Eusebius, suffered torture and horrible death, but being a brave woman, she did not yield quickly to the demands to renounce Christ. Instead, she showed greater strength than her torturers who were exhausted after a full day's effort to break her body and will. Blandine looked at them calmly, smiled and said over and over, "I am a Christian. I am a Christian." And so she died.

In the ironic words of Tertullian, who wrote this bit in his *Apologia*:

> If the Tiber reaches the walls, if the Nile does not rise to the fields, if the sky doesn't move, or the earth does, if there is famine, if there are plagues, the cry is at once: "The Christians to the lion!" What, all of them to one lion?

Fortunately for Western man, the effect of the persecutions, in general, was stimulating rather than destructive—though most painful to the victims, and most disgraceful to the perpetrators.

Arnold G. Toynbee writes:

> But the persecutions of Christianity in the Roman Empire had just the opposite effect to what the Government intended. The Christian Church martyrs have won for the Church

publicity, prestige and converts. In the chaos of dissolving civilization the Christian Church has stood out as something solid and something worthwhile.[1]

---

[1] *America and the World Revolutions* (New York: Oxford University Press, 1962).

VII

THE FOURTH CENTURY A. D.—
THE GREAT DIVIDE IN
WESTERN CIVILIZATION

The trail of private generosity for the public good now arrives at a great divide in the life of Western man—the fourth century.

The fourth century deserves this designation—"the great divide"—because it witnessed the end of the pagan Roman Empire; it witnessed the beginning of the Christian Roman Empire; it was the century of Constantine the Great, the first Christian emperor (311 A. D.); and it ushered in a long succession of Christian emperors.

The fourth century was the age of St. Augustine and his *City of God*; of St. Jerome and his first translation of the New Testament into Latin; of Ulfilas who converted the chiefs of the savage Goths to Christianity and, thus, saved the churches of Rome from destruction a century later, when the savages entered the capital city as conquerors.

It was the century in which the Roman Empire was split in two, and Constantinople was founded to serve as the capital of the Empire of the East.

It was the century in which persecutions of the Christians were ended, and the Christian faith became the recognized religion of the Roman Empire around the whole of the Mediterranean basin.

It was the century in which St. Patrick planted the cross of Christ over the then wild Ireland, and from there sent his missionaries to seek converts in England, Scotland, Wales and western Europe.

It was the age of St. Martin of Tours whose Christian mission to France laid the foundation for French civilization. It was the century in which the first Christian monasteries were established in Europe. They proceeded to send their steady flow of Christian missionaries of faith, education, mercy and healing to millions of peoples who had never previously experienced these civilizing ministrations.

It was the century in which Jesus' original description of his Gospel, that of a life of personal virtue and of kindness to his neighbors, was transformed into the dominant political force in Western civilization.

Last, but not least, the fourth century saw the great transformation in volume and in direction which private generosity experienced. The person-to-person generosity, or alms, began in the fourth century to take the form of institutions of charitable service on a large scale—hospitals, orphanages and leprosaria, houses for the uprooted. Many of these institutions were the prototypes of philanthropic institutions which now exist all over the world.

During the first three centuries, the Christian Church had expanded in number and in influence beyond any valid hopes or dreams. Will Durant[1] refers to its ". . . spread with fluid readiness. Nearly every convert with the ardor of a revolutionary, made himself an office of propaganda."

Tertullian wrote, "Men proclaim that the state is beset with us. Every age, condition and rank is coming over to us. We are only of yesterday, but already we fill the world." By the be-

---

[1] *The Story of Civilization, Caesar and Christ* (New York: Simon & Schuster, Inc., 1944), p. 602.

ginning of the fourth century, it is estimated that there were 7,000,000 Christians; and before 500 A. D. was to be concluded there were to be 15,000,000 living Christians.

CONSTANTINE THE GREAT (311-337 A. D.)

Constantine the Great was born in Serbia in 288 A. D. His father, Constantius Chlorus, was an able and brave Roman general. His mother, Helen, was an innkeeper who became, in later life, a devoted Christian.

Constantius, known as the Pale, or Blond, became—through military victories and personal ability and popularity—Associate Emperor of Rome under Galerius, the emperor. When the Picts and Scots threatened an invasion of England, Constantius the Pale set out at the head of his Roman Army to stop them, having given his teen-age boy, Constantine, as a hostage into the care of Galerius on the Danube. Constantine became restless and asked to be released to join his father, but was refused. Determined to join his father, he mounted his horse in the middle of the night, then set loose all the horses (so he could not be caught) and started a wild ride to the English Channel, joining his father in 306 A. D. at the battle of York in England. The Roman Army won but Constantius the Pale was killed, whereupon the army acclaimed his son, Constantine, as emperor and Licinius the associate emperor. Constantine showed his good judgment by deferring the assumption of this title and responsibility until a valid legal basis for it could be established.

Meanwhile, several powerful politicians plotted against him, including two ex-emperors, Diocletian and Galerius. Finally, deciding to fight against Maxentius, his foremost contender for the crown—or at least for his half of it—he put the Christian monogram upon his banners and defeated Maxentius at the Milvian Bridge outside of Rome. As a consequence, he and Licinius became the emperors in 311 A. D.

Constantine, hailed by millions of Christians in the empire, issued the Decree of Toleration of Christians from Milan in 312 A. D., thereby ending the persecutions. Ten years later when Licinius called for renewed persecutions of the Christians, Constantine canceled the edict and engaged Licinius in battle. Licinius was defeated, captured and imprisoned; but Constantine spared his life.

The pagan Roman Empire was at an end. Christianity became the official religion of the empire, and the pagan symbols and temples began to be destroyed or converted to other uses —all under the rule of Constantine who ruled alone until 337 A. D. and was baptized a Christian on his deathbed.

THE PAGAN ROMAN EMPIRE BECAME THE CHRISTIAN ROMAN EMPIRE

Every Roman emperor to follow Constantine in the fourth century was a Christian, save one—Julian, the Apostate—and he reigned only two years (361-363 A. D.). Disliking Christianity, he knew he could not hope to reinstate the old paganism, so he invented a new Mithraistic form of worship. He wisely appropriated the practice of charity from the Christian religion because he knew it was very popular; but his new paganism did not catch on, even with that inducement.

Julian's failure in establishing a homemade pagan religion is not unlike a committee of students who were religious rebels and who went to a university professor to ask his advice as to how they might start a new religion which would satisfy contemporary young people. The professor advised them: "First, contrive to have one of your number crucified; and second, arrange for him to arise from the tomb and resume his preaching mission."

Each of the emperors who succeeded Constantine the Great in the fourth century (except Julian, the Apostate), issued decrees which granted special privileges to Christians and which forbade pagan practices. In 380 A. D. an imperial order removed the Statue of Victory from the altar in the Senate in order to placate the Christian senators. It had been the symbol of Roman glory since the reign of Augustus. The next to the last emperor in the fourth century, Theodosius the Great, issued the Theodosian Code, summarizing the numerous imperial decrees of the fourth century which relate to the Christian Church and the clergy.

Obviously, the fourth century Christians strove for public as well as private morality. Hundreds of years earlier, Jesus introduced into the world his message of "The Kingdom of Heaven," which led many of his contemporary followers to think of this kingdom as a political kingdom. They asked him when and where it would come? What it would be like? How could one know it? When could one expect it? Jesus denied all interest in that kind of a political kingdom. He preached moral, not political revolt. He specifically commanded His disciples to "render unto Caesar the things that are Caesar's, and unto God the things that are God's."

He said over and over: "The Kingdom of Heaven is *within* you." Following this precept, the primary concern of the Christians in the first three centuries was with the character, ideals and moral standards of the individual Christians, and was not at all with a political realignment. Now, in the fourth century, the Christian Church found itself thrust into the very forefront of a new political and social world, with vast administrative powers which it had not sought.

Constantine and his Christian successors as emperors of Rome decreed many measures aimed at ending injustices and iniquities and at giving the Church authority in many civic duties. Crucifixion was ended as a form of execution. Bishops were obliged to take over certain duties in public welfare, to provide food and shelter for the needy poor and to visit the prisons frequently to check on the justice and humanity of the treatment of prisoners. In some synods the prisoners had to be supplied with their needs from church funds. Constantine gave bishops the status of judges of the courts, and they were given responsibility for seeing that justice was done.

THE CHURCH BECAME A STATE WITHIN A STATE

The Christian Church became "a state within a state," and ultimately the Christian Church absorbed the Roman Empire.[2] The state lost influence. It also lost the respect of the people and split up into smaller groups. What the state lost, the Church picked up; and soon the Church took over much of the political and civil responsibility of the period.

Some theologians believe that the Christian faith suffered almost mortal wounds in the fourth century through the elevation of the Christian Church from a minority "third race of men" to the dominant majority and to the status of a "state within a state." They may be right; it is a matter of conjecture. No one can know what the future of Christianity might have been if it had continued in its pre-Constantinian nature.

But there are also competent historians who believe that Western civilization would not have survived if the strong fourth century Christian Church had not been on hand to hold society together as the Roman Empire continued to disintegrate.

By the middle of the fifth century, the Roman emperor in the West ruled only Italy, and later in the same century he even lost the title of emperor. These historians believe that had not the fourth century Christian emperors made the Church stronger than the state itself, Western civilization of the fifth and sixth centuries would have been completely submerged and annihilated by the conquering hordes of barbarian invaders.

The fourth century was, in truth, one of the great divides in the general history of Western man. Yet, in spite of the upheavals and divisions, the fourth century generosity created

---

[2] See Ulhorn, *op. cit.*

the pattern of philanthropic institutions which we still use in our own 1965 American philanthropy.

FROM PERSONAL ALMS-GIVING TO INSTITUTIONAL PHILANTHROPY

There are several valid explanations for the radical change in the nature of generosity in the fourth century. In the first place, there was a vast influx of new professing Christians. Christianity was now the official religion of the empire; the rulers of the empire were aiding actively in the destruction of pagan worship and were equally active in encouraging the growth of Christianity. It was now popular and safe to be a Christian.

The personal dedication of the alms-giving Christians of the first three centuries was diluted by the millions of new converts, many of whom probably had much less zeal for and knowledge of the virtues and ideals of Christianity.

THE CHURCHES BECAME WEALTHY

In addition, the Church became a wealthy institution; consequently it had more funds in the fourth century than previously, all available to undertake large services for the public good. Churches were permitted to receive bequests, first by Constantine and then by his Christian successors. Some of the emperors themselves endowed the Church, and their example was followed by private individuals. During the Middle Ages it is said that the Church became very wealthy and enjoyed a far greater income from the generosity of its members than any state of Europe had from public sources.

It is possible to explain, and perhaps regret, the changeover from the simple and personal charity of the Christians of the first three centuries to the larger philanthropic institutions, the prototypes of which were created in the fourth century. But the social and humanitarian need for these institutions cannot be denied in a world which was crowding large populations into its cities and towns. Friendly charity suffices when and where the environment of life is simple, friendly and neighborly; but it requires organization and social tools when civilized life becomes more complex.

So it was during the fourth century that new social needs became obvious to the generous Christians, and they created new philanthropic apparatus to serve the public necessity. It is to their credit that they created lasting patterns of philanthropy that are still in use 1,500 years later.

HOSPITALS—FABIOLA, 350 A. D.

Fourth century Christians noted that there were no places for expert care of the sick and injured, so they began to build hospitals. A lady is credited with the honor of having created the first public hospital in Western civilization in 350 A. D. She was Fabiola, a Christian lady of Rome, a member of one of the most distinguished patrician families of that city.

The Fabian family claimed descent from Hercules, the most famous of Greek heroes; and on the maternal side from a daughter of Evander, son of the legendary Greek god, Hermes. Evander was one of the earliest settlers in the city of Rome, on the Palatine Hill. He is said to have introduced to Roman culture several civilizing arts, including the art of writing.

Fabiola, born about 310 A. D., became a Christian and was active in the Church. She had an unfortunate marriage, having a husband who was dissolute and a wastrel.

Fabiola dedicated her life to the sick and poor and used much of her fortune to set up a hospital, the first such institution in the history of Western man. She personally nursed the patients and set the example for other ladies to serve in like devotion.

St. Basil the Great, Bishop of Caesarea, created a similar hospital in 359 A. D. in his city. Soon the hospital became an essential institution in the see cities of the Christian Roman Empire. These fourth century creations of Fabiola and Basil became the embryonic prototype of the thousands of modern hospitals which serve mankind in all sections of the world.

FOUNDLINGS, LEPERS, STRANGERS, CHURCHES

In the Roman pagan world, there was a vicious practice of "exposing" unwanted babies. They either quickly died or were rescued by kindly neighbors. All of this motivated the Christians to establish foundling homes with their own money.

Lepers were outcasts, to be avoided; but Christians remembered Jesus' concern for the unfortunate lepers. So it was that St. Basil created the first leper asylum ever known—at Caesarea. Many followed in other cities.

There were many homeless persons on the move. This social factor led St. Pammachus to found a refuge at Ostia, Italy. A wealthy Christian mother, Paula, and her daughter, Melanie, founded others at Jerusalem; and the Council of Nicaea decreed that one should be created in every city—a kind of fourth century Salvation Army.

The greatest basic product of philanthropy in any century is the religious institution itself—Jewish or Christian—the mother of all "love for God and for mankind." Without the mission of the Church in teaching, exhorting and worshiping, the springs of generous charity dry up and the practice of charity shrivels and subsides.

Fourth century Christian leaders knew this and devoted a vast amount of their charitable resources and zeal to building and supporting churches. In that century, Christian art and architecture had its small beginning. According to Hendrik van Loon,[3] the first Christian Church art arose about 390 A. D. in the little church of San Vitale in Ravenna, then capital of the western Roman Empire.

ABLE FOURTH CENTURY LEADERS

The fourth century produced many able men, in several fields; but most of the best-remembered names were leaders in the spiritual, religious, philosophical and philanthropic fields,

---

[3] *The Arts* (New York: Simon & Schuster, Inc., 1937).

rather than in the fields of politics and war. Indeed, one would be hard put to recall without research the name of any Roman emperor of the fourth century other than that of Constantine the Great. On the contrary, names of other fourth century men come more easily to mind from the rank of bishops, philosophers and missionaries: St. Augustine, St. Jerome, St. Patrick, St. Martin of Tours, St. Basil, St. Chrysostom. It was from the minds and spirits of such men that Western civilization received new motivation, new direction in the century of the great divide.

THREE GREAT CHRISTIAN STATESMEN OF THE FOURTH CENTURY

Fourth century Christians did more than build new churches for themselves. They also converted and trained for leadership great missionary statesmen who were destined to win thousands of others to Christianity and to launch whole nations into the mainstream of Western civilization.

Among these fourth century statesmen were Ulfilas, who inaugurated the civilizing processes of the Gothic German tribes; St. Martin of Tours, from whose life historians date the French nation; and St. Patrick, who planted Christian civilization on the farthest west reaches of Europe-Ireland.

The Teutonic nations can only be understood through an understanding of the fierce and feared tribes of the Goths. They became, after the refinements of Christian civilization, one of the essential segments of the path or conduit of generosity and charity which trekked from Galilee to America.

The Goths were a Teutonic people who first occupied the eastern area of what historians call Austrasia; that is, Central Europe. The Goths probably were of Swedish origin and it is supposed that the earliest Goths came from the Gotland Island in the Baltic Sea at the mouth of the Vistula River. Presumably, they came up the river and made their homes on the eastern section of that vast expanse of forest, valleys and mountains. As time went on, they spread westward and organized themselves into numerous tribes, under their own chiefs. Those tribes in the eastern section came to be called Ostro-Goths and those tribes in the western expanses were known as Visigoths.

Their first contact with Roman civilization was on the eastern front. They frequently ravaged Greece and even Asia Minor as far east as the Black Sea. In 247 A. D. the Goths crossed the Danube River in a raid, perhaps near the present city of Vienna, culminating in a great victory by the Goths over the eastern Roman army, and bringing death to Emperor Decius.

In 276 A. D. the Goths had pushed eastward as far as Pontus on the Black Sea, but other tribes of the Franks and Alemani, who were part of the Roman army, forced them back.

In 321 A. D. Constantine the Great, then Emperor of Rome, repulsed fresh raids by the Goths, forcing them to give up their struggles for expansion toward the Orient. However, a significant event occurred in their military ventures against Constantine and the Christian faith. A great Christian missionary of that day, Bishop Ulfilas, who went with them as they receded back into their native forests converted their chief and thousands of their number to Christianity. He stayed with them, patiently developed a written language for these untutored people and translated the Bible into their new language.

In the following century Gothic tribes entered Rome and took over the control of Italy and of the whole western Roman Empire. Their chiefs announced that they were Christians, but since they were Arian and eastern Christians they were less welcome in Rome. Nevertheless, their native cruelty and crudity had been greatly refined by the practice of Christian mercy and morality.

They were able, energetic, intelligent people—in spite of long generations of savage life behind them. They responded readily to the evangelizing messages of the Christian missionaries, accepted Christian baptism, built churches, assumed the obligations of Christian charity and morality, developed a written language, trained teachers and established schools for their children, and built political units of government. In time, they regrouped themselves in states and nations which gave shape to medieval Europe, the birth of which histories are disposed to date at about 800 A. D.

Ulfilas

Ulfilas (a Gothic name meaning Little Wolf) was born in 311 A. D. of parents who had been captured years previously by the Goths as they raided their native land, Cappadocia, in Asia Minor. His parents were kept captive for the balance of their lives in the forest lands north of the Danube.

At the age of twenty-one, Ulfilas was sent by the Goths on an errand to Constantinople, not far from his parents' native land. While at Constantinople he became a Christian. Longing to take the Gospel back to his friends in the Gothic forests, he was ordained a bishop and returned to his home where he attacked the pagan worship of images and gods so effectively that the chief of the Gothic tribe began a persecution of Ulfilas' body of Christian followers; whereupon Ulfilas requested Constantine's permission for his followers to migrate to Moesia, now known as Bulgaria.

Ulfilas succeeded in three remarkable undertakings. First, he persuaded his colony to give up war. As a precaution he even left the Books of Samuel and Kings out of the Bible which he translated, lest his followers find delight in the stories of the battles in those books. Secondly, he persuaded his colony to settle down into the life of a farming community, to till the field and harvest their crops by their own labor. Up to that time Goths had lived by war and plunder, always leaving the hard work of the farms to captives whom they had enslaved by war. Thirdly, Ulfilas created an alphabet for a Gothic language, a language which up to then (370 A. D.) had been spoken only. Next Ulfilas proceeded to translate the Bible into written text, thereby originating Teutonic literature. Was he perhaps a godfather of Goethe, Chaucer, even Shakespeare?

The conversion and service of this Gothic leader deserves attention because a chief of Ulfilas' Visigoth tribe, Alaric, besieged and captured Rome only ten years after the close of the fourth century—in 410 A. D.—and took charge of the western Roman empire as a Christian rather than as a pagan, a fact attributable to Ulfilas. These people, the Goths, provided a very substantial element of the blood and brains and character of the Anglo-Saxons who first brought Western civilization to America in the seventeenth century.

St. Martin of Tours

Martin was born in Pannonia (Jugo-Slavia), the son of heathen parents. His father, a military officer, required Martin to enter the army at the age of fifteen. Earlier, at the age of ten, he had followed a crowd into a church, merely out of curiosity, and had been much impressed. According to one story, a shivering beggar asked Martin for help, thereby motivating Martin to slash his military cloak in two, giving the beggar half of it. That night, so the story goes, Jesus appeared to him in a vision half-clad in the piece of cloak which Martin had given the beggar. As a result, Martin was baptized a Christian and gave up his military career.

He joined Bishop Hilary at Poitiers and from that time on gave his whole energy and devotion to Christ and the Church. The people of Tours, France, inveigled him to that town and made him their bishop. He created a monastery on the bank of the Loire River and set about evangelizing Gaul by planting monasteries throughout Gaul. They became a refuge for the poor and oppressed, as well as theological seminaries whose monks were in demand in all sections of Gaul. Countless churches and institutions are named for St. Martin who is commemorated by the Church on November 11.

It has been said of St. Martin that he set in motion the energy and the spirit which ultimately created one nation— France—out of the crushed people of Gaul. Modern French historians date the starting point of France from the date of his death, and call him "the founder of Roman Catholic France."

St. Patrick of Ireland

St. Patrick, the patron Saint of Ireland, was born in southern England about 389 A. D., the son of a deacon and the grandson of a presbyter of the Christian Church. In his teens he was carried off to Ireland by a band of Irish marauders, and was kept in captivity there tending the herds of a chieftain. During his six years of bondage, he had religious experiences and visions which led him to flee to the coast and board a vessel belonging to traders who were taking a consignment of Irish wolf-dogs to Gaul. Upon arrival, he walked—for two months— to the Mediterranean and entered the monastery of Lerins. There he studied for a few years before returning to his home in England where he had visions which called him to a life of missionary service in Ireland.

In order to prepare as a missionary, Patrick went to Auxerre and was ordained deacon by Bishop Amator, whence the Pope sent him to Ireland in 432 A. D.

Patrick and his companions proceeded to establish several churches and a monastery for each clan. They also challenged the pagan worship of idols and opposed the Druid festivals. He became the Bishop of Armagh, organized dioceses, converted the tribes that ruled Ireland, introduced the use of the Latin tongue by the Church and through his leadership and personality made Ireland a nation. He died about 461 A. D. and was buried at the site of the first church which he established in Ireland—Saul.

Two centuries later, St. Patrick's church in Ireland was called upon to render a crucial service to England and to western Europe. The fierce and pagan English invaded what later became England from their home on the Continent; forced many residents into the northern and western hills; set up several small "kingdoms," and greatly damaged the churches which had been established in the early years of the Roman

Empire. In the seventh century the Christian Church was re-founded in England. Missionaries were sent there from two directions: To the south they were sent from Rome by Pope Gregory the Great, and to the north they were sent from Ireland by the church which St. Patrick had established there.

Pope Gregory reported that his "forty monks" had baptized 10,000 of the invading Anglo-Saxons in the first two years. The missionaries from Ireland were equally successful in the north. Thus, subsequent generations of each of the four nations of the British Isles were taught to "love thy neighbor as thyself," and were trained in the practice of private generosity for the public good, as were their fellow generations in the other nations of Western civilization.

MONASTERIES

Among the important philanthropic institutions which were created in the fourth century were the monasteries in the west. Frequently, the fourth century hospital, the xenodochium, the monastery and the other charitable structures stood side by side, with the monks residing in the monastery serving the needy in the other institutions.

The key to the spread of monasteries in the fourth century may be found in the desire of some devout Christians to re-create the simple environment and society of the earlier earnest Christians, before the infiltration of large numbers of new converts who had joined the Church when Christianity became the recognized religion of the empire. It has been said that the leaven of Christianity never completely penetrated this mass of new Christians who suddenly came into the Church.

As a consequence, some who were in deeper earnest about their Christian life withdrew from the crowd to live apart in small groups as monks in a monastery, or as nuns in a convent.

Monasteries became a power in the western part of the empire before the end of the fourth century, and developed into one of the most effective and far-flung agencies of Christian evangelism, charity, learning and teaching. Christian monasticism had developed in the early fourth century in the eastern desert wilds of Syria and Egypt. Some of the monks had become unsocial, even fanatical and repulsive in their solitary days and years of penance. Mark Twain has immortalized some of these fanatics. Simeon Stylites is remembered for what seems to be his silly penance, remaining for thirty years on top of a column erected on a mountain near Antioch.

But in the western area, the monastery served very useful purposes. It did not confine its program to the solitary contemplative life, but took up very practical duties as missioners, teachers and friends of the poor, the sick and the needy.

St. Benedict of Nursia, Italy, 480-543 A. D., who founded an early order in the West, imposed poverty and manual labor upon those who took the vows, creating the slogan: "He prays who works."

This pioneer was born in 480 A. D. at Nursia near Spoleto, Italy. After the usual education for a youth of that period, he withdrew from community life and took up his abode in a cave on a mountainside at Subiaco. A friend, a monk in a nearby monastery, brought him food—enabling Benedict to stay in seclusion for three years in prayer, contemplation and austerity. After emerging, disciples flocked to him, assisting in the formation of twelve monasteries in the neighborhood with twelve monks in each. He then led a small band southward and established a monastery on the lofty summit of Monte Cassino, near Naples, the now-famous Benedictine monastery known to all American soldiers who served in Italy in World War II. For centuries it was a chief center of the religious life for western Europe.

These monasteries spread, first throughout Italy, and then into all of northwestern Europe. The Benedictines were dedicated to education. Students were not only trained as future monks, however. Schools for boys who were not planning religious vocations were attached to many Benedictine monasteries. St. Augustine, a Benedictine, and his forty companions planted Christian churches throughout Germany, Holland, Poland and all Latin Christendom.

One of the specific services for which all civilized persons are grateful to St. Benedict was the preservation of Latin literature and history which was copied over and over by hand in his monasteries. Each large monastery also had a library and a school. It is estimated that "90 percent of the literate men (of western Europe) between 600 A. D. and 1100 A. D. received their instruction in a monastic school." [4]

Many other monastic orders were founded in the following centuries, for both men and women. Each of them had a charitable vocation and mission—some for acts of mercy, some for education, some for being friends of the poor, some for care of orphans, some for evangelism, and so on.

A typical order established many monasteries or houses in different sections and nations. Thus, over the 1,600 years since the fourth century beginnings of Christian monasticism in the West, literally millions of members of these catholic orders have given their lives in complete devotion to the spiritual and cultural nurture of Western man. Many of them have also gone as missionaries from the West to all other lands in the world.

Arnold Toynbee, famous historian of our generation, made a pilgrimage in 1953 to the ravine near Subiaco, Italy, where St. Benedict received his call to his Christian vocation. As he read the inscription on the tablet placed there by Pope Pius IX on which were the names of all the lands on Earth which had been evangelized by the impetus that flowed from that humble spot, Toynbee termed it the "Period Germ-cell of Western Civilization" and "prayed that the spirit which had once created a Western Christian civilization out of the chaos of the Dark Ages might return to reconsecrate a Westerning World." [5]

---

[4] Norman F. Cantor, *Medieval History* (New York: The Macmillan Company, 1963).

[5] Arnold Toynbee, *An Historian's Approach to Religion* (New York: Oxford University Press, 1956).

VIII

GENEROSITY PIONEERED

EDUCATION IN EUROPE

(400 A. D.-1500 A. D.)

I^t was the Christian Church which infused into the arteries of Western man during the first four centuries the doctrine and practice of private generosity for the public good. For the first time in the history of mankind millions of persons were taught that it is "more blessed to give than to receive," that one should love and serve his needy neighbor.

At the close of the fourth century (the Great Divide) thousands of small churches with 10,000,000 living members, each member professing his belief in and his practice of generosity, were a vital force. In each church a minister was given the responsibility for ministering to the needy, the poor, the sick, the blind, the forgotten, the old and feeble, the abandoned infant. These Christians in the fourth century set in motion the processes which soon covered the globe with many institutions of mercy and generosity.

Generous charity was ready in the year 400 A. D. to undertake still greater services to the refinement and civilizing of Western man. Within the next thousand years Christian generosity pioneered every cultural and civilizing advance made by Western man.

It is of special interest to note that these massive civilizing achievements were made during the very period of the rapid decline and fall of the political Roman Empire. In 410 A. D. the Visigoths under Alaric captured Rome and sacked it; troops seized everything of value, but respected the "Churches of the Apostles of St. Peter and St. Paul as holy and inviolate sanctuaries." And in 476 A. D. Odoacer, king of a group of Teutonic tribes, captured Rome again and notified the eastern emperor at Constantinople that the western empire was ended.

In spite of these political upheavals of the fifth century, the Christian Church proceeded with the most massive endeavors to create agencies of culture and civilization which it had ever attempted.

The path of philanthropy across the centuries of Western civilization from 400 A. D. to 1500 A. D. leads to—and through —the educational institutions, teachers and tools which were provided for the refinement of Western man by Christian charity, and generosity.

It was inevitable that the Christians of these centuries should realize that one of the ultimate sources of human misery, frustration and suffering is ignorance. They had gained rich experience in the pivotal fourth century in the creation of useful institutions of humanitarian services; now, they turned more of their creative philanthropic zeal and resources to increased efforts to broaden their educational processes.

Greek and Roman culture was declining, professionalism dominated the gymnastics curriculum in Greece, the older standards of morality and sportsmanship were ignored and corruption and bribery became so rife that the Olympic games were abolished in 394 A. D. In 385 A. D. Emperor Theodosius had destroyed the Serapeum in Alexandria and in 529 A. D. Emperor Justinian closed all pagan schools and withdrew all grants of public funds for pagan education.

This is not to imply that the people of the Roman Empire of the first three centuries had no interest in education. They did provide instruction for the children of the patrician and free classes, though not for the children of all families.

Rich men hired tutors to teach their young children in their homes. Elementary proprietary schools were set up for their sons to enter at the age of seven. Slaves or Greek freedmen were hired to teach them—at the cost of about fifty cents per month per pupil.

A few secondary schools were set up, also on a private enterprise basis. This instruction was largely by lectures. Rhetoric and oratory were emphasized. Of course, this type of education reached only a comparatively small proportion of the children of the Roman Empire of that period.

In this vacuum, Christian charity, in its enlarged philanthropic dimensions, began to create educational processes, agencies and tools which served Western civilization for many centuries.

Christians of every century on every frontier have had an instinct for pioneering in education. They give themselves to the educational process with dedication wherever they go, right up to the doorstep of America, where 150 of the first 180 colleges established in the U. S. A. prior to 1860 were founded and maintained by Christian Church bodies.

ELEMENTARY AND GRAMMAR SCHOOLS

The earliest schools (in the third century) were "catechumal" schools which were organized by the Christian bishops for religious instruction only. In the next century scholarly church leaders organized catechetical schools, primarily for the Christion instruction of pagans of the learned classes who became interested in Christianity.

ABBEY SCHOOLS

General education began to be provided for boys about the fifth century. Bishops of the larger cathedral churches added an abbey and appointed an abbott as a teacher of general courses. (Home courses of instruction were created for girls.)

A course of three liberal arts—grammar, dialetic, rhetoric—

was developed; it was called the "trivium." An advanced course called the "quadrivium" was developed in geometry, arithmetic, music and astronomy. Christian charity also pioneered the first English school in this manner.

When Pope Gregory the Great sent the Benedictine monk, Augustine, and his forty monks to England in 595 A. D. to establish the Christian Church in southern England, he selected a strategic site, Canterbury, which was at the crossroad of the several routes to the southern seaports of England and which was also the metropolis of the Kingdom of Aethelbert, the fourth Saxon King of Kent.

An ancient church stood here, St. Martins, in which Queen Bertha, already a Christian, worshiped; Augustine was given permission to establish a Benedictine monastery in St. Martins in 597 A. D., and he was consecrated the first Archbishop of Canterbury in that same year.

It was soon time, therefore, in Pope Gregory's opinion, for Christian charity to begin its pioneering in education in England; so in 601 A. D. he sent an abbot and a grammar school teacher, Mellitus, to Canterbury for that purpose.

Mellitus arrived and was consecrated the first Bishop of London. In 619 A. D. he was made the third Archbishop of Canterbury. St. Martins School was founded in 627 A. D. Thus, it was another "first" in the educational pioneering of Christian generosity along the path of philanthropy, leading from Galilee to the U. S. A.

TEXTBOOKS AND TWO EDUCATORS

With regular courses of study adopted, it was necessary to produce suitable textbooks and to train good teachers. The fifth and sixth centuries faced those requirements, and Christian generosity provided the tools and the teachers through the channels of the Church. Two of these teachers—Cassiodorus and the Venerable Bede—rendered to Western civilization a unique service.

Cassiodorus (490-575 A. D.)

Cassiodorus, a monk and a scholar who aided greatly in providing teaching tools and methods for the early schools which were established and maintained by the Christian Church, was a Benedictine at a monastery which had been established on Monte Cassino; and like his friends, St. Benedict and Pope Gregory, he was devoted to the educational mission of the Church.

Odoacer who ruled Italy as a vice-regent for the Roman emperor in Constantinople, was a Christian of the Eastern or Arian variety. His rule was a moderate and successful one, but worse times were ahead for the West. The Vandals had sacked Rome a few years earlier, and the Ostrogoths and Lombards would be there again before many years should pass.

Cassiodorus and other responsible leaders knew this. He and others did all they could to protect and preserve the intellectual and spiritual values during the stormy years that threatened.

Cassiodorus belonged to a wealthy patrician family, Syrian in origin, which had settled in northern Italy. When he saw the barbaric rule of the Lombards gathering strength, he founded a monastery on his family's private estate with his own fortune and enrolled a body of monks in an order fashioned after the discipline of the Benedictines. He promptly began a great collection of manuscripts of Greek, Roman, Hebrew and Christian literature and set his monks to studying them and making copies of them. He also initiated a collection of all known devices of science; his monks made sundials and preserved other rudimentary mechanical scientific achievements of the past, to be passed on to the future.

Of perhaps still more interest, Cassiodorus wrote a series of school texts for use in the trivium and the quadrivium courses. He was a lighthouse at a time of storm and peril, one of the truly generous men of all Western civilization, who not only "loved his neighbor as himself," but loved and served the future children and grandchildren of his neighbors down the generations of all subsequent Western civilization.

The Venerable Bede (673-735 A. D.)

The Venerable Bede was the first to reckon Western civilization from the birth of Christ. He helped to produce the textbooks, the motivations and the methods of teaching during those centuries in which the Christian Church was pioneering educational institutions for Western youths.

He was a monk of Jarrow on the Tyne in England whose mission in life was to master all the learning of his day; to teach it to 600 monks who were his pupils in his monastery and to numerous visitors who came to hear him; to produce textbooks for their use, and to send them out to teach thousands of others throughout all Britain and western Europe. He left forty-five volumes of his writings at his death which were widely used throughout all Europe.

Bede's textbooks were in all the fields of liberal arts and sciences. His *Ecclesiastical History of England* is still regarded as the chief source of knowledge of ancient England, but his chief interest was in the Christian religion, which led him to produce translations of portions of the Bible in English, the last of which, the Gospel of St. John, he completed on his deathbed. According to one account, his breath began to fail him, so his associates urged him to stop, but he replied, "I don't want my boys to read a lie, or to work to no purpose after I am gone. Take up thy pen and write quickly."

"THE TWO GREATEST EDUCATORS OF MEDIEVAL EUROPE"

H. G. Wells's unequivocal assertion in his *Outline of History* that "the two greatest educators of medieval history were Charlemagne and Alfred the Great," a startling statement though it may be, requires a few facts concerning the service each of these men rendered to Western civilization through general education.

First, it is important to note that each, Charlemagne and Alfred, strode along the path of Christian charity and generosity. Each used the Christian Church as the chief conduit for his educational plans and programs. To be sure, each was the ruler of his people—Charlemagne, King of the Franks and later of the entire Holy Roman Empire; and Alfred, King of Wessen, England. Hence each had access to public funds for his educational program. But government, as such, had not yet taken responsibility for general education, since education in the eighth and ninth century was still in the pioneer stage. And the pioneer in education, as in all other civilizing forces of Western civilization, was the generous charity of the Christian Church.

Charlemagne

Charles Martel had saved Rome when he stopped the Moslems, as they tried to capture Rome and dominate Europe, after they had conquered Spain and had pushed through France as far as Tours. When the Pope asked Charles Martel for military help against the invaders, Charles responded and defeated them in 732 A. D., driving them back behind the Pyrenees, not to bother western Europe further.

Charles Martel's son, Pepin, was chosen King of the Franks by the Frankish nobles in Soissons in 751 A. D., uniting France and Germany for a hundred years.

Pepin's son, Charlemagne, was born in 742 A. D. and became King of the Franks in 771 A. D., reigning until his death in 814 A. D., having been crowned the first emperor of the Holy Roman Empire in 800 A. D.

The western Roman Empire had been dead for generations; the Byzantine or eastern Roman Empire in the East was in decay; the only structure remaining was that of the Roman Church. Consequently, the papacy, in the absence of a strong political structure such as the Roman Empire had provided, became a substitute power—and at times even had to call upon the military power of friendly kings for support.

It was in this situation that Charlemagne (who was familiar with the writings of Augustine) began to think of himself in terms of St. Augustine's *City of God*. At the same time, a new pope, Leo III (795 A. D.) also began to think along these lines. In a move to accomplish the fact, Pope Leo invited Charlemagne to Rome for Christmas prayers (800 A. D.). As Charlemagne arose from the altar, the Pope placed a crown on Charlemagne's head and declared him Caesar Augustus, emperor of the Holy Roman Empire.

Thus the Roman Empire, which had been dead for over 300 years in the West arose as the "Holy Roman Empire" in 800 A. D. It did not, however, meet the expectations of Charlemagne and others so that it would fulfill St. Augustine's muse of the *City of God*. Quite certainly it did not become Jesus' Kingdom of Heaven which "is within you."

There is no dispute about Charlemagne's great service to education. He was sincerely devoted to his "City of God," the Holy Roman Empire, and was keenly aware of the need for educated citizens of that "city." He also knew that education among the Franks and Germans of that period was at a very low ebb, caused as the shadows of the Dark Ages had fallen across the land.

Charlemagne was determined to revive education, so he persuaded Alcuin—an English clergyman whom he met in Rome —to take charge of this revival among the Franks. Alcuin— who had been educated in the Bishops or Cathedral School of York, England, and who became the head of that school— gave his entire energy to the revival of education under Charlemagne's leadership. Later he became head of the Academy of the Palace where he had the king's sons and the young clerics of the chapel as his pupils; he founded the palace library; and he wrote educational manuals, a grammar and other textbooks.

In 794 A. D., Charlemagne recalled him to France and gave him the great Abbey of St. Martin at Tours where he headed the Abbey School to which hundreds of boys flocked for instruction. Undoubtedly, it was Alcuin's educational genius and energy which gave Charlemagne the reputation as an educator which H. G. Wells conferred upon him. Under Charlemagne education was revived, enlarged and strengthened among the Franks in the midst of the Dark Ages.

Alfred, the Great

It is the view of many historians that no monarch of England was equal to Alfred, and that no king ever so richly deserved the characterization of "Great" as Alfred did.

His service was varied and of unique value: He broke the Danes' hold on England; after a series of wars, over a period of thirty years, he drove the invaders off and thus saved Western civilization from the danger of becoming a pagan Scandinavian power. And after their defeat, the Danes ceased their raids which had destroyed numerous monasteries in the British Isles and in port cities in western Europe.

Alfred was a wise and just administrator, known invariably as "Protector of the Poor." He was a scholar and a teacher who reorganized the ruins of learning and education wrought by the Danes. At the same time, he established a court school and imported scholars from the Continent and from south Wales. He also translated and published numerous books which provided the base for the revival of philosophy, history, verse and literature for the England that arose after him. For example, he translated Boethius' *Consolation of Philosophy* which became the most popular textbook and manual of philosophy of the Middle Ages; he edited an anthology of selections of wisdom, literature and poetry from many sources, chiefly from St. Augustine, called *Blostmon* or *Blooms*.

Alfred founded two or three monasteries to take the place of those destroyed by the Danes and imported foreign monks to study, teach and serve. In addition to reviving the knowledge of Latin among the clergy, he translated into Anglo-Saxon many portions of the Bible. Furthermore, he converted Guthrum, the Danish King and twenty-nine of his leaders to the Christian faith when they withdrew from their efforts to subjugate England.

In regard to his translation of the Bible, Alfred made known his wish (which, incidentally, has been passed down from one English generation to another) that "all freeborn youth of his kingdom should employ themselves on nothing till they could first read well the English Scriptures."

Alfred's own soliloquy, in *Blostmon,* sums up his contribution:

> Therefore he seems to me a very foolish man, and very wretched, who will not increase his understanding while he is in the world, and ever wish and long to reach that endless life where all shall be made clear.

THE FOUNDATION OF THE UNIVERSITIES

One of the most far-reaching philanthropies of the centuries was the founding of the first universities in Western civilization. Essential as they were and are to civilized man, there is no evidence that the early universities received any support, financial or otherwise, from the political state during the early creative generations. The university of Western man appears to be a shining example of "pioneering generosity." The founding and support of the first universities was left entirely to the private initiative of individuals and the agencies of the Christian Church in the early centuries. Most of these universities in Europe are now the proud possessions of their national governments, which exercise jealous control over them—this is probably as it should be, for private generosity is essentially a pioneering servant of humanity!

Higher education in Western civilization had informal beginnings, and the earliest university life was modeled after life in the cloister of the monastery—though the students were not members of a monastic order. The teachers, however, were frequently, though not always, Benedictines, Dominicans, Augustinians, Franciscans and later Jesuits.

Frequently students, and some teachers, passed from one university to another, thus creating a sort of free confederacy of learning, without state control.

The earliest universities in the West are recorded in this order: Salerno 850 A. D. (chiefly noted for its medical faculty) —it did not survive; Bologna 1088 A. D.; Paris 1130 A. D.; Oxford 1150 A. D.; Cambridge 1190 A. D.; Padua 1222 A. D.; Salamanca 1234 A. D.; Prague 1347 A. D.; Cracow 1364 A. D.; Vienna 1365 A. D.; Erfurt 1370 A. D.; Heidelburg 1386 A. D.; Cologne 1388 A. D.; Leipzig 1409 A. D.

Bologna University

Bologna, 1088, is regarded as the chief progenitor of Western universities; a sort of *alma grande mater,* for it did exert a strong influence upon subsequent universities. Present professors at Bologna have reason to believe that some of their early teachers and graduates were active in the founding of the University of Paris, which was chartered a generation later and which became the model for all the other early universities of Central Europe and England.

Bologna was a loose collection of student guilds in its early years; its instruction was chiefly in the law, canon and civil. Schools of theology and medicine were added later, as was that of philosophy. Its first students were of mature years—many of them were archdeacons, canons of cathedrals and heads of schools. The teachers (women served on the faculties from time to time; an innovation not generally followed again for several centuries) taught their students in their own homes, and the students lived as boarders where landlords would have them. Numbering 10,000 students by 1260, Pope Pius IV ordered the cardinal legate, Carlo Borromeo, to erect a building for the university in 1562.

Two students—famous to this day—studied at this university:

Dante in 1287, the great Christian poet; and Petrarch in 1325, the famed poet and humanist.

Note: The greatest treasure in Bologna's museum is Raphael's painting of St. Cecelia, the noble Christian martyr of Rome, the heroine of one of Chaucer's *Canterbury Tales,* referred to in Chapter VI.

University of Paris

The University of Paris took its rise out of the teachers in the Cathedral of Notre Dame. For security's sake, Paris was originally a small settlement on a little isle (called the "Ile de la Cité") in the Seine River on which Notre Dame now stands in its full glory.

The Chancellor of the Cathedral licensed members-of his staff as teachers. After some years their teaching spread to the left bank, also, and the university came formally into being between 1150-1170. Its first written statutes were completed in 1208, and its legal charter was granted in 1211 by authority of Pope Innocent III. This charter may have been the prototype of our Western corporation, for it gave the university a separate corporate entity with the privilege and responsibility for its own order and discipline, and the right to sue and to be sued. By the fourteenth century, the university had become a federation of forty colleges, with each college governed as a religious or secular group of students and teachers.

The Sorbonne

The Sorbonne is the most common name for the University of Paris, named for Robert de Sorbon (born at Sorbon, France, in 1201) who became a well-educated theologian. As chaplain to Louis IX he gained the esteem and patronage of that pious ruler, enabling him to establish Le Communauté des Pauvres Maîtres Etudiant en Theologia (The Society of Poor Masters Studying Theology). No wonder they shortened it to "The Sorbonne"! It became the first endowed college, and along with the other three faculties of the University of Paris, set the pattern for universities in western and northern Europe.

Cardinal Richelieu, whose seventeenth century church is still a part of the Sorbonne in Paris, is known as the second founder of the Sorbonne through generous grants akin to those of the original founder.

Oxford and Cambridge Universities

The University of Paris provided the model for the other universities of Central and Northern Europe, and for Oxford and Cambridge.

The path of generosity now, temporarily, crosses the English Channel where Christian generosity provided the financial means and the manpower to set up the two great universities in England.

Oxford University grew, over the years, out of the teachings of the abbot and his masters in the Osney Abbey which was in the see of the bishopric of Osney and Thame in the Diocese of Oxford. Osney lies just outside the walls of the present university and is the site of the magnificent Augustinian foundation which overlooks the university wall. Teaching had also centered around the dissolved nunnery of St. Frideswyde at Oxford.

Robert the Prior—a scholar and teacher—had visited Rome several times; he translated an abridged Pliny and dedicated it to King Henry II. As was the case at Bologna and Paris, a small community of scholars and teachers began to assemble and by the early years of the twelfth century this community took on the characteristics of a university. It lists its founding date as 1150 A. D.

In the years 1167 and 1168 numerous English students, who had been studying at the University of Paris, came back to England and were admitted to Oxford at a time when France and England were having one of their periodical quarrels. King Henry II ordered all clerics who were at the University of

Paris on income derived from English churches to return to England. At the same time the King of France expelled all alien students from France.

Thus Oxford and Cambridge Universities had considerable additions to their young institutions, all because—as this event evidences— Christian charity was helping young men to obtain a higher education.

In the early years, the Bishop of Lincoln appointed the Chancellor of Oxford University; later he was elected by the masters. Among early scholars or lecturers at Oxford were Roger Bacon, Duns Scotus, John Wycliffe and Erasmus.

A few years after Oxford University was founded, the Dominican, Franciscan, Carmelite and Benedictine orders established communities in Oxford; and the members of these orders "profoundly affected the advancement of learning in many lands."

Cambridge University is given the founding date of 1190 A. D., and there is no doubt there was teaching of sorts going on in Cambridge during the twelfth century. The reputation of the teaching was good enough to attract a number of students from Oxford University in 1209 when instruction was interrupted at a time at Oxford due, it is said, to some serious disputes between "town and gown."

Cambridge University was patterned after Paris University, as Oxford had been. It had a chancellor who was recognized by the King of England, and the Pope at Rome. His appointment had to be confirmed by the bishops of Ely until the middle of the fifteenth century. By this time, the mendicant orders had made Cambridge the center for their educational missions in eastern England.

Among its famous teachers were Erasmus, Cranmer, Tyndale and Sir Isaac Newton.

Like Oxford University it was sustained and supported by Christian charity, first by the Roman Catholic Church and later, after Henry VIII, by the Dissenters, Puritans and other Protestant bodies.

Emmanuel College

Two extremely important events took place in the decade of 1580. One of these events, in 1587, has made headlines in all the histories of Europe and the West, namely, the defeat of the Spanish Armada in Spain's attempt to invade and subjugate England. It marked the fortunate end of the effort of the Spanish throne to dominate the Western world.

The other event made no headlines, then or now; but it too was extremely important to all mankind; it was a bridge-head on the path of generosity. It was the founding of Emmanuel College at Cambridge University in 1585 A. D. by Sir Walter Mildmay, Chancellor of the Exchequer in Queen Elizabeth's government.

Sir Walter was a Protestant, a Puritan. Queen Elizabeth was the head of the Church of England. While she had great respect for her Chancellor of the Exchequer as a businessman, and a loyal cabinet member, she did not find it advisable to discuss their religious differences.

Sir Walter decided to make a gift out of his own fortune— to found a new college at Cambridge University, which would be useful in instructing its youth in the doctrines of the free choice of religious faith and the supreme worth of the individual. He absented himself from court for a day to go to Cambridge and dedicate the new college. When the Queen noted his absence and requested an explanation, Sir Walter replied, "Madam, I have been away planting an acorn, and when it becomes an oak, God only knoweth what it will amount to." The term "acorn" proved to be a good forecast of the future role of Emmanuel College at Cambridge University.

The Reverend John Harvard was one of the early graduates of Emmanuel. He came to New England at the age of twenty-nine, and began to dream about a college like Emmanuel for his new home. Two years later he died, leaving his library and one-half of his small estate, which he inherited from his father, a "green grocer," for the proposed college. With this aid the institution was soon founded at Cambridge, Massachusetts. It received his name and in 1642 the first class was graduated from Harvard College, only thirty-seven years after Sir Walter planted his acorn—Emmanuel College—at Cambridge University.

Graduates of Harvard College helped to found Yale. Harvard and Yale graduates helped to found many of the other great American Colleges across the whole breath of our nation. All of these early colleges were expressions of the consuming desire of generous men and women to provide sound higher education for the sons and daughters of a new nation.

Dr. Norman Vincent Peale—Minister of Marble Collegiate Church, N.Y.

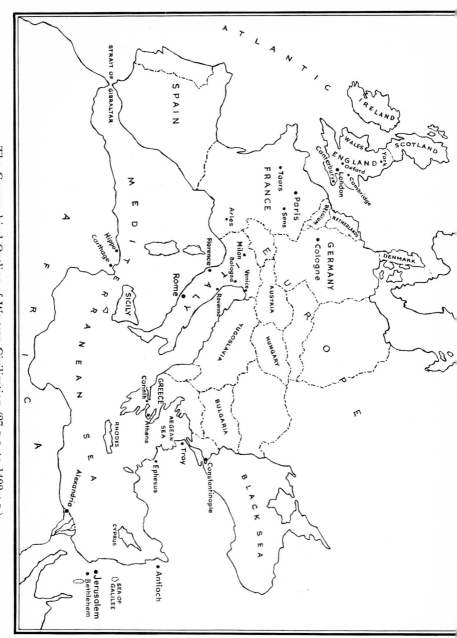

The Geographical Outline of Western Civilization (27 B.C. to 1492 A.D.).

Ruins of the Roman Amphitheater where the great public spectacles were staged.

Chapel in the Church of Ste. Cecilia Metellus which was erected in Rome as a memorial to the martyred "Sainte of Music and the Blind." She was immortalized also in Chaucer's *Canterbury Tales*.

The First Christian Church Art (Church of San Vitali, Ravenna, Italy—built about 390 A.D.).

King Alfred the Great of England (848-900 A.D.). While traveling incognito, he was scolded by a peasant housewife for letting her cakes burn while he sat daydreaming.

The Richelieu Church—the
Sorbonne of the University of
Paris, 1150 A.D.

Bologna University, Italy. Founded in 1088 A.D., it was the first permanent university in Western civilization.

Within less than a century after the first Gothic Cathedral was constructed in France, the English erected this Gothic Church at Salisbury in 1220 A.D.

Christ Church College, Oxford University, England. Founded by Cardinal Wolsey, 1525 A.D.

Cologne Cathedral (Germany).
Begun in 1298 A.D.—completed
in the nineteenth century.

Emmanuel College, Cambridge University, England. Founded by Sir Walter
Mildmay, 1585 A.D.

The Last Supper—Leonardo DaVinci's most famous Christian painting.

The ancient refectory in Milan—on the plaster wall of which Leonardo DaVinci painted The Last Supper.

IX

THE DEVELOPMENT OF
THE ARTS IN WESTERN
CIVILIZATION (500 A. D.-1500 A. D.)

There is no question about it—the Christian Church served as the conduit of private generosity during the first five centuries of Western civilization. In those early centuries private generosity extended a hand of sympathy and helpfulness to neighbors who were hungry or homeless or in prison or sick or forgotten. It developed the first humanitarian institutions which dispensed mercy, health, loving care and shelter to those in need of such ministrations.

Later this generous concern of man for his fellow man created schools, trained teachers and provided textbooks for the education of youth.

It was to be only a matter of time until the satisfying of new desires and capabilities for the refinements of life through the development of the arts of painting, architecture, sculpture, music, literature, calligraphy and illumination was to become a part of this same generosity.

As Kenneth S. Latourette states: "It was largely through the Church that the fine arts were kept alive and developed."[1]

---

[1] Kenneth S. Latourette, *History of the Expansion of Christianity*, Vol. XXIX, *The Thousand Years of Uncertainty: 500-1500* A. D. (New York: Harper & Brothers, Publishers, 1938).

ARCHITECTURE

Along the path of Western civilization, the period of 500-
1500 A. D. displays the fruits of generosity of Western man in
the Romanesque and Gothic cathedrals. The designing, the
engineering, the sculpturing genius and the brains were provided chiefly by the monastic orders and their sub-order of lay
architects. The "pioneering" money was provided by the Christian Churches of the synod and by the weekly offerings of all
the members. The tools were hammer and chisel and crowbar
and winch and rope; the muscle was that of the sturdy peasants
who dropped their own work at the call of the bishop.

First, there were the small village churches made of stone,
with a simple nave and bell tower, built by the peasants with
their own labor and with their own generous offerings. Stone
is underscored, because that was part of the charm and magic
of the churches in a generation when the people lived in houses
and shacks made of wood. But God's houses were made of
stone, they were loved and admired by the populace and they
were not easily destroyed. Some of them are still to be found in
remote valleys of Europe to this day.

Romanesque Cathedrals

During the period 750 to 1150 A. D. the bishops' churches
and cathedrals were built in the Romanesque style. This
beautiful architectural pattern was developed to a high degree
in the eighth, ninth, tenth and eleventh centuries. They com-
bined features of the Roman basilica, of Byzantine art and of
quite new and creative features which varied in different sections of Europe and the British Islands. These features were
often meaningful, mute sermons in themselves. On the columns
was the sacred tree of life with some carvings depicting animals; some depicting fruits; some, vegetation; some, the human form; and some were carvings of Biblical allegories.

A striking feature of the Romanesque church was the use of
vivid colors of many hues. Unlike the later Gothic cathedrals,

the walls and ceilings of the Romanesque church were made resplendent with brilliant blue and green figures and designs. Early Romanesque cathedrals were erected at Portiers in the sixth century, at Ravenna, Fulda (791-822 A. D.), at Aix La Chappelle (795 A. D.), at St. Gall (850 A. D.) and at Cologne (850 A. D.).

Gothic Cathedrals

The artistic genius of Western man became more creative as the generations rolled on, reaching a high point in the twelfth century in the Gothic cathedral which looms majestically over the path of generosity in Western civilization.

Several legends survive about the origin of this unique style of architecture. One says it is an artistic reproduction of the towering pine trees under which the Gothic tribes had camped in their period of barbarianism.

Van Loon[2] rejects this as a fable and says that the Gothic cathedral was created for the narrow-walled city where real estate was at a premium (for reasons similar to the erection of our modern sky-scrapers), while the Romanesque cathedral was created for the agricultural area where the architect could spread his structure out over wider spaces. Whatever the reason, it is true, of course, that a distinctive feature of the Gothic cathedral is its emphasis upon vertical lines. This contributes to the sense of height which seems to lift the sharp lofty spires up to heaven.

The Romanesque architecture developed into Gothic architecture in the twelfth century in a manner which professionals in the arts regard as natural and complementary. Its impressive feature—its use of vertical lines—contributes to the sense of height which is rather dizzying at times to one on the ground directly beneath. But the ability of these lofty spires to command views from long distances is inspiring, even thrilling.

It was during the twelfth century that the first Gothic church,

---

[2] *Op. cit.*

the Abbey of St. Denis in Paris, was completed (1144). And it was in the same century that the first Gothic cathedral, St. Etienne, was begun at Sens, France (1140), though it was not completed until 1562.

The consecration of the Gothic abbey church of St. Denis (on Montmartre, Paris, and named for the first bishop of Paris) was an event worthy of the birthday of Gothic church architecture. Nineteen bishops and archbishops consecrated the altars.[3] (A Gothic cathedral could have thirty altars, and some later ones did.) King Louis VII was present as the Lord's Annointed, and King Henry played the part of Christ at the consecration while twelve of his knights played the parts of the twelve apostles.

Other Gothic cathedrals were: St. Etienne, Sens, which stimulated the use of the Gothic in other lands and provinces (its choir was copied as far away as the Cathedral of Canterbury in England); the Chartres Notre Dame Cathedral, built on Gothic lines in 1194-1220; Notre Dame, Paris, 1163-1240; the Notre Dame at Amiens, 1218-1269; St. Mary at Salisbury, 1220; Lincoln, 1255; Duomo, Florence, 1298 (completed in 1898, after many variations); Santa Croce, Florence, 1350; Rouen, "Lace in Stone," 1400-1504.

CATHEDRALS PIONEERED BY CHRISTIAN GENEROSITY

These noble and impressive symbols of art, refinement, culture and spiritual exaltation were pioneered and initially financed by the generosity of the Christian Churches and people, marking a notable forward thrust of Western civilization. They became so popular and meaningful to the spirits of Western man, that before long princes and kings were vying with the Church in building more and finer cathedrals and in filling them with precious treasures.

Funds for their erection were provided in many ways, after the pioneering had been done by the Church. A state, a city or a monarch might make a grant from the public treasury;

the bishop might provide the funds; the people might be appealed to for contributions, or the funds might be raised by a combination of these and other methods. All the great cathedrals were, in part at least, built by freely donated labor. At times—as when heavy masonry was to be lifted to the towering spires—the people of the whole countryside would drop their work for days or weeks at a stretch to carry and haul and pull the ropes. Some of these massive structures were 200 and 300 years in the building. When completed, they became great repositories of Christian art—treasure houses of the finest paintings, sculpture, stained glass, tapestries and precious metals produced by the European masters. For centuries they were, undoubtedly, the central factor in the cultivation of the Western world's appreciation of the arts.

(An interesting sidelight on the exquisite workmanship of the artists who helped to create these cathedrals comes from scholars who have researched the agricultural life of medieval Europe. In their efforts to determine just what the popular products of the farms, gardens, vineyards and orchards of that period were, they have found some important information in the carvings of fruits, vegetables and flowers on the pillars of the cathedrals of the era.)

PICTORIAL ART

Just as pioneering generosity aided architecture in creating its cathedral masterpieces in the twelfth to fourteenth centuries, so it aided the amazing outburst of pictorial art in the fifteenth and sixteenth centuries.

In that period some of the greatest artists of all time produced masterpieces which to this day inspire, uplift and amaze Western man. The artists were commissioned by the Christian Church to create their masterpieces, and they selected as their subjects the personalities and the events of the Hebrew and Christian scriptures, and the Church gave them the gallery for the display and custody of their beautiful creations.

Leonardo da Vinci

Son of a lawyer in Florence, Leonardo da Vinci was a painter, sculptor, architect, musician, mechanician, engineer and natural philosopher. Born in 1452, a legend declares he was the last man in Western civilization who mastered all knowable knowledge, so declared because learning and science were advancing so rapidly that no man after him was ever able to master all knowledge.

Leonardo began his greatest Christian painting, "The Last Supper," in 1494. It became the most impressive and most famous representation of the scene in which Jesus and each of his twelve apostles appear. It has been, and still is, one of the most precious treasures of all Christendom. Leonardo painted it in tempera on the plaster wall of the refectory of a convent in Milan.

Over the centuries, this rough room has been abused (it was once used as a stable) and the plaster has flaked. Misguided efforts were made many times to repair and restore it by artists who assumed it was an oil painting. The ghost of the picture was finally brought back to life in the nineteenth century by a skillful artist, Cavenegho, who loved and understood it. Prints and lithographs have been manufactured and distributed in unknown quantities to many generations of Christians and other art lovers.

Leonardo da Vinci exerted a great influence upon Western civilization. His genius was nurtured and supported financially by the Christian Church, the mother of Western man's generosities.

Michelangelo

Michelangelo—a native of Florence, an artist, a sculptor, an architect—was born in 1475, the son of a "poor gentleman." At the age of thirteen, he knew he wanted to be an artist. His preference was for sculpture, but he was first obliged to study the painter's art. He was apprenticed to a painter at the age of thirteen, then transferred to the School of Sculpture of Lorenzo in the Medici Gardens, where he was an ardent student of Dante's poems.

He completed the famed colossal statue of David, carved out of one huge block of marble, in 1504. Pope Julius then summoned him to Rome and ordered him to execute a series of paintings in the Sistine Chapel—most important of which was the decoration of the ceiling, a work which remains his chief title to glory. To complete the work—a design of hundreds of figures which embody the story of Genesis from the creation to the flood—he worked incessantly, face up and on his back, for four and one-half years. By 1513 the masterpiece was finished. Then, he created one of the most famous examples of sculpture, the gigantic figure of Moses, now in the Church of Peter in Chains in Rome.

Ten years later, in the 1530's, he completed one other famous sculpture, "La Pietà" (Mary, the mother of Jesus, holding the body of her son who had just been crucified on the cross). It was this sculpture which Pope Paul VI loaned to the New York World's Fair (1964-1965).

Michelangelo was recalled to Rome by Pope Clement (1554) to resume his paintings in the Sistine. He settled in Rome for the balance of his life, and began another of his great Christian sermons in oils and colors: the "Last Judgment," perhaps the most famous single picture in the world. Its only competitor for the distinction is "The Last Supper." When completed in 1541 the artist then turned to his other great frescoes "Conversion of Paul" and "Martyrdom of St. Peter."

During the last years of his life he turned to the art of architecture in which he also excelled, having been appointed chief architect of St. Peter's Church, responsible for the remodeling and embellishing of it. The dome of St. Peter's as it now stands, is one of his noblest achievements. Michelangelo died in his ninetieth year (1564).

Michelangelo stands along the Path of Generosity because his artistic contributions were made possible by the support of the Christian Church.

Raphael

Raphael Sanzio—the painter whose popularity has never been excelled—was born in Urbino, Italy, the son of a painter. His religious paintings are hung in the Vatican and in many great museums—the Louvre, the Metropolitan, the Victoria and Albert, the Petti, the Uffizi, the National and a score of others. Among his most famous paintings are: St. George and St. Michael; St. Paul preaching at Athens; the Coronation of the Virgin; several paintings of the Madonna; the Holy Family with the Lamb; the Entombment of Christ, and others.

Raphael was invited (1508) to collaborate in the creation of the new Church of St. Peter at the Vatican by Pope Julius II, who gave him the responsibility of designing many of the famous frescoes that enrich the majesty and beauty of the Vatican. Later, Pope Leo X appointed Raphael inspector of all excavations in and near Rome, including the catacombs. Consequently, Raphael is on the Path of Generosity because his achievements were made possible by the Church which retained him and supported him from the generous offerings and gifts of its worshippers.

Music

The Christian Church made much use of music from the very earliest years when even in its small group services (held in the homes of members), hymns of praise were sung. Music was included in the educational curriculum of the early bishop and grammar schools. Many hymns—"plain songs"—had been composed by members while living in dark refuge in the catacombs of Rome. In 314 A. D., Bishop Ambrose of Milan set a body of these tones in order for use in worship. Later, Pope Gregory the Great (600 A. D.) revised and enlarged Ambrose's tones in the Gregorian chants.

During the time Charlemagne served as emperor of the Holy Roman Empire, he arranged for church music to be taken to the Germans and Franks north of the Alps; and upon his request, the Pope sent "music missionaries" to establish schools of music at Metz and St. Galls.

Organs also were sent along by the Church, the first to be used in Germany. All of these developments were the result of Christian generosity, pioneering the cultural life of Western man.

Palestrina

Music was a little later in its renaissance than were pictorial art and architecture. During the early centuries of the Renaissance Church, music lost some of its quality, due, it is said, to some "silly music." The Roman Catholic Church was put on the defensive in the sixteenth century and the Council of Trent was called (1545-1563) to try to set its house in order. Among other things the council studied was the state of church music.

Fortunately there was a musician and composer of great talent who had the utmost devotion to the Church, Giovanni Palestrina (1526-1594), who had been brought to Rome and entrusted with several important duties: Magister Cappelae, St. Peters; singer in the Sistine Chapel; the Vatican choirmaster of the Church of St. John Lateran, Rome. The Council of Trent asked Palestrina to write new music for the masses. The result was a simple and pure form, which convinced the authorities that polyphonic music could be devout. Among Palestrina's other compositions were a book of "Magnificato" for all the Ambrosian tones; and a book of "Lamentations" for use in Holy Week.

Thus, music soon resumed its rightful place in the culture of Western man. Some of the greatest musical compositions of all time were produced in that area which Charlemagne had seen to be in need of music seven centuries previously. Two great early composers of that area, born in the same year (1685) in Germany, were Bach and Handel.

Johann Sebastian Bach

Born at Eisenach, Germany, Johann Sebastian Bach came from a family which had been preeminent in music for 200 years. Beginning his career in music as organist and composer as a boy, he later wrote colossal compositions on themes from the Bible: *The Passion According to St. Matthew; The B Minor Mass; The Christmas Oratorio; The Magnificat; The Kyrie and Gloria Masses.* These are a few of the priceless musical treasures of Christian devotion which Bach contributed to the onward flow of civilization in the West. As with other "greats," he deserves to be placed on the Path of Generosity, because his whole career had been made possible when the Church had sent missionaries of music to Germany several centuries before his birth.

George Frederick Handel

Born in 1685 in Halle, Saxony, Germany, George Frederick Handel was the grandson of a barber-surgeon. He began the study and composition of music at the age of eight and was sent to Berlin, for further instruction, at the age of twelve; but his father objected, because he wished Handel to become a lawyer. Handel, therefore, went to the University at Halle as a law student in 1702, and soon became organist of the cathedral. His first opera—*Almira*—was performed in Hamburg in 1705.

Handel turned from Italian operas to chorals and cantatas, choosing Biblical themes: Esther, Deborah, Saul, Israel in Egypt, Samson, Belshazzar. His immortal oratoria *Messiah* was produced in 1742; and his *Hallelujah Chorus,* the triumphant hymn to the risen Christ, has uplifted the hearts and souls of Christians for four centuries. Handel who created his career in the Church, "the Mother of Charity," also walked along the Path of Generosity. The Church in Germany was supported by taxation, at least in part, in Handel's day, but music had been taken to Germany centuries earlier by missionaries from the Church at Rome.

THE PRINTING PRESS AND THE BIBLE SOCIETIES

Before leaving Continental Europe on the Path of Generosity, one more instance of pioneering generosity looms brilliant: a unique philanthropy which followed immediately after the invention of the printing press in the middle fifteenth century, either by Coster in Holland in 1446 or by Gutenberg in Germany in 1454.

As any schoolboy knows, the earliest book which these presses printed in Western civilization was the Bible, in 1456.

The Bible began to flow from the early publishing plants set up in Basle, Venice, Paris, London and elsewhere. It was the "best seller" of that day and of many subsequent generations. It seems to have contained the germs of the great ideas which nurture the spirits and characters of peoples of all races around the world.

Bible societies were set up in the sixteenth, seventeenth and eighteenth centuries by generous men in several nations, to produce Bibles in great quantities and to distribute them free (or at low cost) to millions of persons in all parts of the world. By the close of the nineteenth century the Bible had been printed in 567 languages. These Bible societies were created by private generosity in Geneva, Germany, England, New England, France, Hungary, Holland, Poland, Sweden, Denmark and even Russia.

This sixteenth century generosity has expanded greatly during subsequent centuries, to the point where there are now twenty-three national Bible societies in a world fellowship termed the United Bible Societies.

At least one book of the Bible has been translated into 1,261 languages and dialects, and the whole Bible has been fully translated and published in several hundreds of these languages.

The United Bible Societies published and distributed 55,-000,000 Bibles and portions of Scriptures in 1963. Commercial publishers of Scriptures do not reveal their sales figures, but they probably total many additional millions.

X

PRIVATE GENEROSITY
RESCUED ENGLAND
IN THE FIFTEENTH
TO SEVENTEENTH CENTURIES

The Path of Generosity has led to Ostend and Calais where the view takes in the Straits of Dover and England, the place where pioneering generosity and Western civilization generated new human and cultural values under the aegis of parliamentary self-government.

A glance backward along the Path of Generosity, across Continental Europe reviews the evidences of generosity's pioneering services in the development of civilization's educational, health, religious, artistic and cultural agencies. What a dreary wasteland Europe would have been if generous concern for one's fellowman had not been in the front line of civilization's surge to the West!

Such a backward glance at the Continent is also tinged with some regret, for the high days of pioneering generosity there are ended, never to return—at least it hasn't up to the present.

Europe was a fragmented group of jealous nations, speaking different tongues, worshiping God in a variety of faiths, contending with each other for power and territory. The political leaders superseded philanthropy by nationalizing schools, universities, hospitals, orphanages—even churches, the very mother of generosity—and by financing them with taxes laid on the peoples. Generosity completed its 1,400 year assignment of pioneering Western civilization in Europe. And the new European nations allowed it to go, because their rulers did not want their citizens to exercise the free creative powers of pioneering generosity.

The European nations turned to their major occupation of bloody warfare with each other. The greed of a few of their rulers for greater possessions of wealth wasted much of what they once possessed; and they have slaughtered generation after generation of their choice youths, whose brains and creative energies were desperately needed.

Thus, in the fifteenth century, pioneering generosity says perforce to Continental Europe, "Farewell" and faces westward across the Straits of Dover, with a "Hail, England!" Christian generosity had pioneered churches, schools, universities, cathedrals and other agencies of public service in the British Isles for centuries contemporaneously with its similar pioneering services on the Continent.

Now, however, private generosity was to undertake a far greater pioneering service to Western civilization through the creative initiative of the freedom-seeking, English speaking peoples in the British Isles and in America. In England it was to "form the shape of the modern world."

AT THE EDGE OF SOCIAL REVOLT

England was facing social dissolution in the fourteenth and fifteenth centuries. The peasants were at the edge of revolt; the poor were in despair; the government had not yet sought the legal power to repair the crumbling social structure, and the social conscience of the citizens had not yet been stirred to action.

John Ball, "mad priest of Kent," defied orders and had preached his bitter declarations of the rights of man week after week. For twenty years (1360-1381) he had given utterance to the despair of the poor. It is said that these were the first such sermons in English.

"Good people," he cried from his pulpit, "by what right are they whom we call lords greater folks than we? . . . They have leisure and fine houses; we have pain and labour, the rain and wind in the fields, and yet it is of us and of our toil that they hold their state."

Wat Tyler, the leader of the English insurgents, was assassinated by the Mayor of London in the presence of young King Richard II (1381)—hence his movement collapsed. This revolt of the peasants and of the poor was not confined to England, however. The Continent experienced manifestations of the spirit of despair, too. A group of laborers in the Po Valley, Italy (1200) formed themselves in the "Society of the Humiliati" and appealed for the simplicity of the life of Jesus and his apostles. At the same time, Peter Waldo, a wealthy French merchant, adopted a life of poverty and attracted others who called themselves "the poor men of Lyons."

In addition, Arnold of Brescia gathered a following of labourers in the northern Italian cities in Lombardy in 1300-1400. His "Apostolic Brethren" preached the near approach of the Kingdom of God, of justice, of equality and of peace; and in France in 1358, the French peasants had risen, burnt châteaux and despoiled the countryside. While in Bohemia about 1396, a learned Czech, John Huss, rector of the University of Prague, delivered a series of lectures based upon the doctrines of John Wycliffe of Oxford University. He was burned at the stake, an act which intensified the peasants' revolt, already in progress, in that country. A century later a series of bloody peasant wars swept over Germany.

Poverty in all western Europe and the British Isles had become a normal status of society throughout the middle centuries as the cities and towns had grown larger. Economic causes had produced unemployment and vagrancy in the fourteenth century; the Church was being weakened from within and without, and plagues had disorganized society and terrified the people.

Meanwhile men's minds were beginning to think of the reasons for their misery, and they were beginning to speak out against injustices when they recognized them. There were many manifestations of this fermentation of the minds and spirits of men during the fourteenth and fifteenth centuries, as knowledge spread and as the mustard seeds of the Christian concern for the dignity of the individual burgeoned into new aspirations and hopes.

Many of the men highly placed in the Church at this period were acutely conscious of the distress of the poor and tried hard to bring about a Christian society. Bishops took one step against human slavery, which was practiced everywhere, by decreeing that no Christian could be kept in slavery by another Christian. Dante, Aquinas, Savonarola wrote or preached against all injustices and cruelties. Popes Gregory VII and Innocent III tried to use the Church as the instrument for abolishing the hardships of the common man. But the hour for complete reform for these social ends had not yet struck.

The Christian ethic had stirred the people, but the solution was not yet within their grasp.

Private generosity was to provide a solution for England through the initiative and benevolences of its merchants and bankers.

The growing resistance of the common man against serfdom and a life of unending toil and chronic subservience must surely have been stimulated by the Christian teaching of the worth of each individual, as it was expressed by the Reverend John Ball. The preachers who delivered the message of Jesus, generation after generation, consciously or not, planted the mustard seed in the hearts and minds of multitudes of men; and eventually these seeds sprang up into an overwhelming yearning for freedom, for justice, for recognition of lowly men as sons of God rather than as ignorant clods or two-footed animals of toil.

Poverty and general hopelessness among the English people reached record depths in the fifteenth and sixteenth centuries. The causes of the widespread dislocation of everyday life in

England were numerous and cumulative. Civil and foreign wars ravaged and disorganized the economic order. The weight of over-population, the movements from rural to city life, the changes in agricultural products, the weakening of the Roman Catholic Church (and their monasteries and many charitable agencies) and, finally, King Henry VIII's break with Rome and seizure of all the land, churches and institutions of the Roman Catholic Church—these tore the social fabric of England into tatters.

Families lost their homes; men lost their jobs; thousands of English men, women and children became permanent vagrants. Hundreds of them would roam the countryside and highways en masse looking for jobs that did not exist, living by begging or worse. They became a burden upon their fellows, and a threat to the continued stability of England.

Leaders in churches, universities and parliament began to call for solutions; literature of protest began to pour from the presses; preachers began to sound the alarm from their pulpits. The English conscience was stirred to action—and to this day, the English people have not lost their revulsion to mass poverty and inequity which they were led to feel so deeply in those dark days of social dissolution in the first half of the sixteenth century.

THE PRIVATE GENEROSITY OF MERCHANTS

Fortunately for England, the two Tudor monarchs of the sixteenth century, King Henry VIII and Queen Elizabeth I, were sensitive to social unrest. As the drumfire of pamphlets and the eloquence of the dissenter preachers stirred members of Parliament to legislative action, the King—and later his daughter Elizabeth I, when she became queen—put his seal upon new laws that "put a floor" under the social order which would prevent total collapse.

But this was only a stop-gap. The Tudor Charitable Laws included major sections which encouraged generous men and women to give their private means to supply the needs of the poor and to cure the basic causes of poverty.

A most satisfying account of the salvation of the civic structure of England by private generosity is to be found in the book *Philanthropy in England, 1480-1660* by W. K. Jordan.[1]

Jordan has researched and recorded every gift and bequest made to charities during the period 1480-1660 in a group of ten English counties, which included *more than half of the disposable wealth of the nation.*

After the Tudor Charitable Laws legalized private generosity for the public service of the poor, religious and business leaders took up the responsibility for encouraging men and women to give generously of their means to build and endow schools and colleges, orphanages, almshouses, hospitals, welfare stations and old people's homes. They poured out their funds generously in amounts large and small.

According to Jordan, "The great preachers . . . laid forever on the English conscience a sense of the shame of poverty and a moral responsibility for the enlargement of the orbit of opportunity . . . profoundly and permanently altered the English character and aspirations."

These generous men and women Jordan concludes, "had, it is not too much to say, formed the shape of the modern world."

LATER PIONEER SUCCESSES OF ENGLISH GENEROSITY

English philanthropy did not disappear, nor even subside, after it had helped to "form the shape of the modern world" in the social crises of the sixteenth and seventeenth centuries.

On the contrary, private philanthropy in the next three centuries in England launched some of the most far-reaching humanitarian institutions and movements of modern Western man, demonstrating once again the oft-proved thesis that gen-

---

[1] See also Jordan's *Charities in Rural England: 1480-1660* (New York: Russell Sage Foundation, 1961).

erosity is an expression of the nature of man, rather than a measure of his bank account.

It is quite understandable that persons who have not made any special study of the nature of charitable giving would assume that when a person had made a generous gift for a social need, he would feel he has invaded his financial resources sufficiently and cannot be expected to make other generous gifts.

This, however, is not the typical experience of generous givers. For some reasons, unseen and even not fully comprehended (like most spiritual motivations), many generous givers develop giving as a habit; a pleasing and satisfying refinement; a meaningful expression of personality; a welcomed participation in the effort to create a better and nobler world.

So it came about in England following the upsurge of philanthropy during the Tudor years. It was not a mere flash. The sixteenth and seventeenth century generous men and women had truly reshaped the nation, and had passed on to the next generations the zeal and faith to tackle other social problems and to dedicate their generosity to expanded efforts for a better world.

A NEW WORD FOR CHARITY IS CREATED

The English people were so impressed with this new and powerful force which had been introduced into their national life by their generous charities that they created a new name for it—a name with broader implications and with a greater dignity than the ancient word "charity," which meant to many persons a small alms held out to a supplicant.

The new name—philanthropy—was probably first created in 1650 by Dr. Jeremy Taylor in a sermon he preached in London. A brilliant preacher and author of that day, Taylor served also as "Chaplain in Ordinary" to King Charles I. Taylor's word is now our favorite term for the ancient virtue of charity. It is a pleasant   word—homemade from two Greek roots: *philo* meaning love; and *anthropos* meaning all humanity.

PHILANTHROPIES PIONEERED IN ENGLAND

A few philanthropies, which were founded in England in the eighteenth, nineteenth and twentieth centuries follow—not in any extended interpretation because the service which each pioneered is well known. Each has been of immense scope and depth in its spiritual value to Western civilization.

1775   John Howard and Elizabeth Fry pioneered prison reform.

1780   Robert Raikes of London founded the Sunday School Movement.

1833   William Wilberforce headed the Quaker Anti-Slavery Society, which brought about the Act for Abolition of Slavery in the British Domain.

1844   The Y. M. C. A. was created in London by George Williams.

1854   Florence Nightingale organized and led a corps of nurses in the Crimean War, bringing about the creation of the nursing profession.

1864   The International Red Cross Society was founded in Geneva, as a result of Florence Nightingale's activities.

1865   The Salvation Army was created in London by General William Booth.

1869   The first Charity Organization Society in the world was founded by the Earl of Shaftsbury, Cardinal J. H. Newman, and the Honorable William E. Gladstone.

1885   Canon S. A. Barnet and a group of Oxford men founded the first Settlement House—Toynbee Hall in London.

1885   Baron Maurice de Hirsch of London gave £11,000,000 to establish the Jewish Colonization Society.

1885   Sir Moses Montefiore of London gave large sums to ameliorate the lot of oppressed co-religionists in other lands.

1885   Mission to Lepers—first in the world founded in Dublin and London by Christian Laymen.

1908   General R. R. S. Baden-Powell created the Boy Scouts.

XI

GENEROSITY IN AMERICA

(1620-1965)

The Path of Generosity has led to the impressive scope and volume of the philanthropic, private agencies for the public good in the United States, a generosity that now exceeds $11 billion each year and is still rising.

Private generosity for the public good had commenced in America in the very decade (1620) in which the first settlers had arrived and it became an essential force in our American culture.

The American segment of the Path of Generosity is studded by literally hundreds of thousands of agencies for the public good which were pioneered by the initiative and generosity of private citizens who longed to create this new nation of free men living under parliamentary self-government.

CHURCHES

The first generous zeal of the early settlers in America, from 1620 on, was to build churches and to create programs of worship which were in accord with their respective beliefs.

The Puritans (Congregationalists) in Massachusetts and Connecticut, under the leadership of John Cotton, William

Mather, Thomas Hooker and others, established forms of worship which they had been denied in England.

Churches in America undertook their traditional practices of private generosity for the public good promptly, and for the next three centuries it was the Church which pioneered "nearly every educational and refining agency in the American culture. " If it had not been for the sparkling genius and indefatigable energy of Benjamin Franklin, America's greatest fund raiser, we might properly take the "nearly" out of that quotation.

Some of the most zealous of the early leaders were: *James Blair,* rector of an Episcopal Church in Scotland, who became the rector of the Bruton Church in Williamsburg, Virginia, and the first president of the College of William and Mary.

Francis Makemie, Presbyterian, an Irishman, who labored as an itinerant preacher in Maryland, North Carolina and Virginia, and founded several churches in that area. He was arrested for preaching at Newton, Long Island, and imprisoned for six weeks, tried by jury and found *not guilty.*

William Penn, a Quaker, who obtained a grant of land covering much of the province of Pennsylvania and established Quaker meetings in Philadelphia and the surrounding area— which founded many schools and colleges, and initiated far-reaching social reforms.

Peter Minuit, who came to what is now New York City in 1626, as Governor of New Netherlands. He founded the white settlement on Manhattan Island; purchased the island from the Indians; named the settlement New Amsterdam; and built a blockhouse, a mill and homes.

Dutch Reformed ministers and people who came to New Amsterdam and two years later, in 1628, built their church, called the Dutch Reformed Collegiate Church. During the three subsequent centuries, this church moved up Manhattan Island as the city expanded northward—later it branched into several parishes. The present Marble Collegiate Church has stood at Fifth Avenue and Twenty-ninth Street for over a century. It is the oldest church in America, having a continuous ministry since the date of its establishment. Currently, Dr. Norman Vincent Peale, famous preacher and author, is the pastor of this historical church.

Count Zinzendorf, 1741 and *Henry Muhlenberg,* 1742, who were leaders of the tides of German immigrants who were driven out of their homes in Europe by bitter religious persecutions. They established many churches for Moravians, Mennonites, Dunkards, German Quakers, and Lutherans in Pennsylvania, Maryland, Central New York and Georgia.

Lord Baltimore, Cecelius Calvert, second Lord Baltimore, who received a charter from the King of England in 1632, for the territory which now encompasses the State of Maryland. He colonized it as a refuge for persecuted Roman Catholics, but invited and urged other groups also to come to Maryland. Lord Baltimore's policy was that religious toleration and liberty of conscience should be firmly established in the colony.

Roger Williams, a Baptist, a graduate of Pembroke College, Cambridge, who became acquainted with leading Puritans in England and developed radical separatist and political connections which brought him to the attention of the formidable Bishop Laud. He rightly thought it wise to leave for America, where he arrived at Nantucket in 1620; but his ideas on religious freedom were too radical for even the Boston Congregationalists. Williams was brought to trial and expelled from Massachusetts. He turned to friends, the Narragansett Indians, whom he had befriended in the loss of their lands to the white man; and now they befriended him, giving him a grant of their land on the bay. Here Williams founded Providence in 1632, and the colony of Rhode Island followed, where he established America's first Baptist Church in Providence in 1639.

John Wesley, Methodist, who founded the great Methodist Church in England in 1739. Methodism was brought to America in 1768 by Francis Asbury and other associates of the founder, and the itinerant Methodist circuit rider preachers became a factor of great importance in the development of the nation.

Christian churches have been "The Mother of Charities" for 1,935 years, ever since generous charity was first adopted by Western man in 30 A. D. as a primary virtue. They continued to stimulate private generosity in North America as they pioneered the culture of our nation.

PRIVATE GENEROSITY'S PIONEERING FUNCTION IN AMERICA

Private generosity for the public good has pioneered nearly all of the great social advances in our nation.

The unique pioneering function of private generosity deserves to be more clearly defined and more generally recognized. Too frequently within the present generation, partisanship has been created between those who believe government should take responsibility for all educational, health and welfare services and those who would prefer to see all these agencies under private control. The whole social experience as a nation tells us that we greatly need *all* the educational, health and welfare agencies that both government and private generosity can provide—as a team.

Strangely enough, and much to the surprise of many, the relatively recent support of government for our civilizing agencies has greatly stimulated private support for many of the same causes—and vice versa! The support of private generosity has stimulated government support by arousing legislators to know that the voters value these causes and will approve increased appropriations for their expansion.

There is no other explanation for the geometrical annual expansion of private generosity for public purposes from a total of $1¼ million in 1930 (just before the vast expansion of governmental taxation and expenditures for general social and welfare causes began) to $11 billion in 1965 (when the budget of the federal government alone reached a high of $100 billion).

Many have warned that the "invasion" of government into the area of education, health, the arts and welfare would dry up the traditional zeal of free Americans to give the money and provide the initiative for our private agencies for the public good. In spite of the warning, private generosity for public services has increased as rapidly as has government support for them!

What is the conclusion? That the American people want a greater refinement of life for themselves and their fellows, and are able and willing to support such social advances with both their taxes and their private generosity!

PRIVATE GENEROSITY PIONEERED ELEMENTARY AND SECONDARY EDUCATION IN AMERICA

After the establishment of churches, private generosity proceeded to pioneer schools. It was many years, in fact over two centuries after the first arrivals on the Atlantic coast, before the American states would be willing to legalize the collection of taxes for public schools for the education of their children.

Meanwhile, the earliest settlers began their own private and community schools on their own initiative and with their own money.

The very first school was started in Manhattan in 1638, by members of the Dutch Reformed Church who had arrived from the Netherlands to found the settlement which they called New Amsterdam, and which the British later renamed New York.

It was named the Collegiate School, and for 250 years it was a parish day school for the Collegiate Dutch Reformed Church, later becoming a community grammar school. It is the oldest existing private secondary school in the United States, just nosing out for that honor Roxbury (Massachusetts) Latin School, which was established in 1645.

This early urge of colonial Americans for the education of their children, and their willingness to take the responsibility and to pay the bills for schools can be best explained in their own words. A copy of the statement signed by citizens of Roxbury, Massachusetts, declared their intention to establish the Roxbury Latin School: ". . . in consideration of their religious care of posterity have taken into consideration how necessary the education of their children in literature will be, to fit them for public service in Church and Commonwealth, in succeeding ages. They, therefore, unanimously have consented and agreed to erect a free school in the said Town of Roxbury." The leader of this community generosity, the Rev. John Eliot, minister of First Church, was known as the "Apostle to the Indians."

The following is a list of the fifteen schools which were established by private generosity prior to the Revolution—and which are still active:

Fifteen Schools Established by Private Generosity Before 1776

1638   Collegiate School, New York City, by Dutch Reformed Church.

1645   Roxbury Latin School, Roxbury, Massachusetts, by local citizens led by Reverend John Eliot.

1660   Hopkins Grammar School, New Haven, Connecticut, by bequest of Governor Edward Hopkins.

1689   William Penn Charter School, Philadelphia, Pennsylvania by Society of Friends.

1689   Friends Select School, Philadelphia, Pennsylvania, by Society of Friends.

1697   Abington Friends School, Jenkintown, Pennsylvania, by Society of Friends.

1709   Trinity School, New York City, by Trinity Protestant Episcopal Parish.

1742   Moravian Preparatory School, Bethlehem, Pennsylvania, by Moravian Church.

1742   Moravian School for Girls, Bethlehem, Pennsylvania by Moravians.

1746   Linden Hall, Lititz, Pennsylvania, by Moravians.

1759   Germantown Academy, Philadelphia, Pennsylvania, by private generosity.

1763   Governor Dummer Academy, South Byfield, Massachusetts, by Governor William Dummer.

1764   Columbia Grammar School, New York City, by Columbia College.

1765   Rutgers Preparatory School, New Brunswick, New Jersey, by Queens College (Rutgers).

1774   Newark Academy, Newark, New Jersey.

Approximately fifty more of today's strong academies were founded between 1776 and 1800 and, of course, there were hundreds of other so-called "charity schools" founded and supported during the period of 1650 to 1850 which completely disappeared when states and cities and townships began to provide tax supported schools.

THE STRUGGLE FOR FREE PUBLIC SCHOOLS

It is quite difficult for a citizen of 1965 to understand the bitter struggle for free public education that was waged in the fifty years after our new nation was established in 1787. The agitation for and against free schools went on in every state except in the New England states where the attitudes were more favorable.

The chief battle was over the issue of tax support for the public schools. Several tax schemes were tried and failed: endowments by public lands in the west; lotteries; rate bills. It became clear that special school taxes must be levied; yet, New York and Indiana were especially obdurate, and a member of the Indiana General Assembly closed his emotional tirade against free schools with these deathless words, "When I die I want my epitaph written: *Here lies an enemy of free schools.*"

Private generosity aided directly in this struggle through the instrumentality of public school societies. These were organized and financed by private citizens to help inform the people and the legislatures about the need for tax-supported education.

Massachusetts produced a plan of taxation which finally won in the other states by 1850. It granted the state the right to tax for education and to compel local governmental units to raise an equal amount for education by local taxes. This victory took the burden of elementary schools from private generosity; but the struggle to include the high school as an integral part of the public school system and, therefore, to make high schools the object of tax support went on for another twenty-five years before court decisions gave tax status to secondary education also.

PRIVATE GENEROSITY PIONEERED OTHER EDUCATIONAL AGENCIES

Private generosity did not abandon education, however, when tax support took over the public schools. It never does turn its back on one of its "cultural children." On the contrary, when public tax support is ready to take over the basic support for a civilizing instrument which private generosity has pioneered, the latter nearly always increases its interest and its support by pioneering new extensions and refinements of that agency, which it would be difficult or impossible for public officials to undertake in the experimental stages.

The following are some educational refinements which private generosity pioneered after it saw its "children"—elementary and secondary public education—well settled as members of the family of tax-supported social agencies:

Normal Schools for Training of Teachers. In 1839 Edward Dwight of Massachusetts offered $10,000 toward the establishment of the Massachusetts Normal School, if the state would give a like amount. The result was that three normal schools were started by this stimulus.

Schools for the Deaf. In 1817 the Reverend T. H. Gallaudet founded the Connecticut Asylum for the Education of the Deaf and Dumb. Personal generosity provided most of the funds, and by 1880 there were sixty-one such institutions, about half of them tax-supported. One college for the deaf was founded on the private initiative of the philanthropist, Amos Kendall, and was named Gallaudet College. It is now a federal college.

Schools for the Blind. Dr. S. G. Howe founded the first school for the blind, the Perkins Institute in Boston in 1832, the first of many such schools—some supported by private generosity, some by taxes.

Schools for Mentally Retarded. Dr. S. G. Howe also established the first school for the feeble-minded in Barre, Massachusetts, about 1850—it was the forerunner of many institutions and movements in mental hygiene.

Evening Schools. The Public School Society of New York City, opened the first evening school in 1834, as an endeavor to combat truancy and vagrancy among children. The idea spread quickly and widely in many cities, and soon it also stimulated adult evening education for men and women who were obliged to work for a living during the day, but who were eager to stretch their minds and spirits by evening study.

Kindergartens in 1859, Southern Mountain Schools in 1865, Education for Negroes in 1865, and *Summer Schools in 1874.* Generosity also pioneered these vital extensions of education in the last half of the nineteenth century.[1]

Generous Americans have shown an unmatched zeal and benevolence for groups of citizens who have been overlooked or neglected by mass educational processes. American generosity tries valiantly to pioneer the services which will provide the blessings of a culture in which they are presently not sharing fully. Wise philanthropists welcome the assistance of tax support for such agencies for which a true partnership in motive and purpose can be established.

[1] See Arnaud C. Marts, *Philanthropy's Role in Civilization* (New York: Harper & Brothers, Publishers, 1953).

PRIVATE GENEROSITY PIONEERED COLLEGES AND
UNIVERSITIES FOR AMERICA

Thoughtful Americans of this generation (and of past generations) are fully aware that their national welfare and their very prosperity are directly dependent upon the degree of their intelligence; which, in turn, is directly dependent upon the quality and extent of their education. Man's dependence upon education is far greater today than it has ever previously been. America's fabulous natural resources provided the grist for much of her past prosperity. For generations Americans have been blessed by native wealth in coal, gold, iron, forests, unbounded western farm lands, silver and oil.

This present generation has reason to know that these natural resources do not replenish themselves. We are realizing (too slowly) that we must live upon the production of our brains rather than upon our natural physical resources, and that education, research and creative genius must be trained to produce at least 75 percent of our annual income for the immediate future and beyond.

Obviously, higher education in America is essential to the future sound economy of our nation. Private generosity pioneered the founding of colleges and universities on 2,000 campuses across the land, all ready and eager to perform this new and greater service to the American people.

Our first settlers lost no time in founding their colleges. Quite early, the Reverend John Harvard came to America (from Emmanuel College in England) and helped to found Harvard College (1636) at Cambridge, Massachusetts, thereby initiating the progeny of colleges which were founded in the wake of Harvard. The Massachusetts colony created a unique form of "voluntary" taxation for the support of Harvard. Two men were appointed in each town to visit every household and solicit support for the college. An average tax of one-half bushel of corn was a suggestion made by some of these tax gatherers. Harvard's major support, however, came from gifts, grants, and bequests; sources other than the unique system of taxation.

Dr. Donald A. Tewksbury,[2] claims that 150 of the first 180 permanent colleges in America which were in existence in 1860 had been founded by Christian Churches.

Each college in America has at least one favorite story of the efforts which its early leaders and friends made to bring it into existence, or to keep it alive in its years of poverty and strain. They include the story of the president of a struggling college in Kansas who pushed his way through a New England blizzard to visit a generous man, who was astonished that *any* man would walk the street that night for *any* cause. The college (Washburn College, Topeka, Kansas) now bears his name in gratitude for his timely generosity.

Another college boasts of a devoted man who served a small church college, Heidelburg College, Tiffin, Ohio, in the midwest as a fund-raising agent. He called himself the "College's Fisherman," and he walked the highways of three states each year to call on members of the churches, bringing back many small offerings in silver coins, thereby enabling his college to survive.

Princeton University, which announced in 1965 one bequest of $37 million, rejoices in President Witherspoon's visits to England, Scotland and Bermuda to solicit funds for this college.

Harvard also sent agents to England. It has been said that during some of the early years (before the American Revolution), Harvard received more funds from England than from its friends in America.

William and Mary College sent Dr. James Blair to England, where on the occasion of one of his visits King James I appealed to the churches of England for contributions for this college in America which was then affiliated with the Church of England.

Mount Holyoke College has its story of Miss Mary Lyon who

---

[2] *The Founding of American Colleges and Universities before the Civil War* (New York: Teachers College of Columbia University, n.d.).

traveled many scores of miles to solicit funds for the college, returning with 1,800 subscriptions ranging in amounts of six cents up to a total of $27,000.

All colleges have their own heartwarming stories of generous and dedicated men and women. If all those generous persons were ever assembled in one mammoth panoramic panel it would present a composite portrait of the finest essence of American character and culture.

All of the pre-Revolutionary colleges were founded by Protestant groups. Promptly after our federal government was established, the Roman Catholics also began to establish colleges—the first being Georgetown University at Washington, founded by the Jesuits in 1789. Thirty other Roman Catholic colleges were created prior to the Civil War decade—1860. They included St. Louis University by the Jesuits in 1818; Fordham by the Jesuits in 1841; Manhattanville by the Religious of the Sacred Heart in 1841; Villanova by the Augustinian Fathers in 1842; Holy Cross by the Jesuits in 1843; Notre Dame by the Congregation of the Holy Cross in 1843; and San Francisco by the Jesuits in 1856—to mention only a few.

A few state universities were established promptly after the Revolution—notably Georgia, 1785; North Carolina, 1789; Vermont, 1791; Tennessee, 1794. But higher education, as a whole, was the concern of generosity, church and private, until 1862 when Congress passed the Land-Grant Act. This act encouraged states to create and maintain state universities by offering a grant of western public lands to each state for that purpose. Many states took advantage of this federal aid and established universities, agricultural colleges, mechanical and industrial institutes, and other institutions of higher and specialized learning.

DUAL SYSTEM OF HIGHER EDUCATION

Thus, the American system of higher education became, fortunately, a dual system—*a full partnership between private generosity and government.* There were mistaken prophets, of course, who said the Land-Grant Act tolled the doom of private colleges; that philanthropy would no longer give to higher education, which would look thereafter to the public treasuries. It did not happen that way. The Office of Education of the United States Department of Health, Education and Welfare reveals that there are still 1,078 recognized four-year institutions of higher education in the United States of America which are under independent or church affiliation. In addition, there are 234 more two-year institutions of higher education in these affiliations. The breakdown is as follows:

Church or Independent Affiliation	Number of 4-year Institutions	Number of 2-year Institutions
Independent	386	106
Church Affiliations		
Baptists	74	23
Lutheran	43	12
Methodist	91	24
Presbyterian	64	8
Catholic	264	42
Other Christian	147	19
Jewish	9	0
Total	1,078	234

GIFTS TO EDUCATION HAVE MULTIPLIED BY 151 TIMES

In further evidence of the inaccurate prophecies of 1862, a study of the comparative annual giving to education of that period with that of today, shows that gifts to education in 1870 (nearest date available for comparison) totaled $8,593,000, whereas gifts to education in 1963 totaled $1.3 billion—151 times the 1870 figure! Team cooperation between private generosity and public funds works in the U. S. A.

FIVE PUBLIC SERVICES BY PRIVATE GENEROSITY

Volunteer Fire Companies

Anyone who has ever lived in a village or town can easily recall the excitement experienced, as a boy or a girl, when the whistles screamed, when the church bells rang or when a fire alarm sounded. The community responded—on the double. The men wheeled out the pumper and hose reel; the women made coffee and sandwiches; the older boys formed a bucket brigade, and the young fry had a romp.

This is how the magnificently mechanized and trained city fire departments got their start—as volunteer fire companies. The first one of record was established in 1752 in Mt. Holly, New Jersey, followed by thousands which were organized subsequently—and which still provide the only fire protection for many small communities.

The money needed for the equipment and housing was raised by subscriptions and by all sorts of picnics, bazaars, carnivals, ice cream and strawberry socials, and auctions. It was hard work for many, but it was good community recreation also. At any rate, the volunteer fire company was a manifestation of the American genius for solving a community problem.

The Hospital

Hospitals in America had their very earliest beginnings in connection with "pest houses" for sailors with contagious diseases (Manhattan 1663) and Alms Houses (Philadelphia, 1731), but these early wards were not for the general public.

Probably the earliest general hospital established in the United States was Charity Hospital in New Orleans (1737)—it is still surviving. It was started by a gift of $2,000 from Jean Louis, a sailor and later an officer of the East India Company. Forty years later, it was destroyed by a storm and rebuilt by private generosity; but it is now owned by the state.

It was Benjamin Franklin, of course, who solicited some

private pledges (he always had a pledge card with him) and worked out a smooth "matching offer" with the Provincial Assembly to establish Pennsylvania Hospital in Philadelphia in 1751.

New York City's first general hospital, New York Hospital, was founded by private generosity in 1770, and was helped by support from the Municipal Assembly and, later, from the State of New York.

Boston Dispensary was founded by the Reverend Samuel Parker and associates with private gifts in 1796.

The Free Public Library

There are two heroes in the history of America's free public library system—the irrepressible Benjamin Franklin and the doughty Scotsman, Andrew Carnegie.

It was Franklin, of course, who founded the first library when he and his associates, The Philosophical Society, created a library for the free use of the public. His example was followed by generous public spirited citizens in Charleston, Providence, New York and Baltimore. There was considerable resistance to such a luxury in Massachusetts and it was not until 117 years later that the State of Massachusetts passed an act which permitted a municipality to tax itself for the support of a library.

Private generosity labored a century and a half in patient demonstration of the value of public libraries before the general citizenry was ready to vote tax support for them. It was Andrew Carnegie who turned the tide early in the twentieth century by his offer to thousands of cities to pay for a public library, if they would support it thereafter. The reaction of the canny Scots of Edinburgh was quite similar to that of canny taxpayers in the United States. During a referendum in Edinburgh for a proposal to finance a library building, the voters were induced to vote, "No" by the display of signs which read,

Rate payers!
Resist this Free Library Dodge
and save yourselves from the burden of £6,000
of Additional Taxation

Five years later Carnegie offered Edinburgh a free gift of
£50,000 to erect a library building—and the voters accepted!
The library was built.

It then came about in the U. S. A., and Carnegie's offer was
accepted by numerous cities. Libraries sprang up all over the
land, in what has been termed "a noble American epidemic."
Carnegie gave $60 million for 2,811 libraries.

Museums

Museums were also introduced in the United States by private generosity. The earliest museums, still in existence, include:

1803	The Museum and Art Gallery of the New York His-torical Society.
1805	The Pennsylvania Academy of Fine Arts.
1807	The Boston Athenaeum.
1825	The Yale School of Fine Arts.
1826	The National Academy of Design.

Later, municipalities, states and the federal government developed a great variety of museums and voted the funds for
partial or full support of them.

Smithsonian Institute, one of the greatest museums in the
United States, was founded by the will of James Smithson, an
Englishman who never saw America. He left $500,000 in 1829
to the U. S. Government for the founding of the institute.
Congress finally accepted the bequest and now votes generous
supports for its program.

Smithson was clearly desiring a suitable memorial. He chose
wisely, declaring: "The best blood of England flows in my
veins; on my father's side I am a Northumberland, on my

mother's I am related to kings, but this avails me not. My name shall live in the memory of man when titles of the Northumberlands and the Percys are extinct and forgotten."

Medical Research

Medical scientists of every generation have devoted their energies, their knowledge and their skills in efforts to discover the reasons for the physical and mental suffering caused by sickness, malfunctioning, contagious plagues and the many other incidences of human suffering.

Prior to the twentieth century, "The Generous Century of Western Man," the medical scientists who elected to dedicate their energies to the war on disease, fought their battles with the very minimum of scientific equipment and staff support, in part at least, because their financial resources were most limited.

Private generosity in America provided the missing "money factors" in the twentieth century by bringing previously undreamed-of financial support to the medical scientists. As a consequence, the medical and allied professions have achieved victories over the ravages of human disease in the first sixty years of our century which might well equal, if not exceed, the progress made in this area of human well-being in all the previous centuries of Western civilization.

The story is an exciting one. It cannot yet be told, because the forces of research which were released early in the present century by private generosity are still rising steadily. It will be a very pleasant duty for future historians to tell the story of medical scientists versus preventable human suffering in the twentieth century.

The Rockefeller Institute for Medical Research

The creation of the Rockefeller Institute for Medical Research in 1902 must surely be regarded as the crucial breakthrough in the twentieth century assaults by scientists upon preventable diseases. It was established under dignified professional leadership; it had very substantial financial support from America's most generous family; it was able to attract the brains and enthusiasms of top-ranking scientists; it reflected prestige and respect upon the very concept of "medical research." Nothing was the same in this field after the advent of the Rockefeller Institute for Medical Research.

The preliminary action took place in 1897.[3] It grew out of an association between John D. Rockefeller, Sr., and a Baptist minister, Frederick T. Gates, whose wise counsel on philanthropic and educational matters was a positive factor in many of Rockefeller's generosities.

Gates read—in the summer of 1897—a textbook by the famed physician, Sir William Osler, entitled *Principles and Practices of Medicine*. Gates was fascinated by Osler's account of the neglect of medical study and education in the United States. He had sensed this educational deficiency in the field of health and medicine. He called this situation to the attention of Rockefeller, recommending the endowment of studies and research in the health fields which would free a staff of physicians and scientists from the practice of their profession and enable them to devote their abilities to study and experimental research.

In 1901 Rockefeller made his first gift of $200,000 for medical research, thereby creating the Rockefeller Institute for Medical Research. Dr. William H. Welch of John Hopkins University was made president of the first board of directors.

The next year Rockefeller gave $1,000,000 for a site and construction of a laboratory, and his son John D. Rockefeller, Jr., was active in selecting the location on Avenue A, between Sixty-fourth and Sixty-seventh Streets. Dr. Simon Flexner was appointed Director of the Institute. Soon the medical and allied scientific professions began to experience illuminating transfusions of new knowledge and to find available to them new techniques and stimuli.

---

[3] Cf. Raymond B. Fosdick, *John D. Rockefeller, Jr.* (New York: Harper & Brothers, Publishers, 1956).

The completed researches of the institute were published in scientific journals or issued as monographs, and later assembled into volumes, being distributed to institutions of education, laboratories and scientists in all sections of the world.

Over the years, Rockfeller gave the Rockefeller Institute for Medical Research over $60 million. The Rockefeller endowments have continued generous support for the Institute which pursues its service to mankind with unabated zeal and skill.

Rockefeller's generosity aided and stimulated almost every element of human well-being, and he was interested in all phases of his humanitarian generosity. But a friend is reported to have said to Rockefeller that his two greatest successes "were the founding of the Rockefeller Institute for Medical Research and the training of his son."

Doctors and scientists were given new stimulus and encouragement to intensify their efforts to reduce the ravages of killer diseases. Within ten years after the Rockefeller Institute for Medical Research began to distribute the published reports in its researches, the medical profession and generous citizens organized a half dozen national committees, each of which was aimed at one of the major diseases then afflicting mankind. Within the next half century these national committees against named diseases reached a total of more than forty.

The first such national committee to be created was aimed at the disease which had been the principal cause of deaths for ages—tuberculosis. The National Tuberculosis Association was founded in 1904, mounting an assault on the number one killer of man. The association achieved its goal; it continues the fight through 2,162 state and local committees who raise over $30 million per year from the generous public for research and other costs of the continuing fight.

In 1908 doctors and public spirited citizens founded the National Society for the Prevention of Blindness; in 1913, the American Cancer Society was launched; and during that early decade, seven permanent national committees against specific afflictions began their work.

In the 1920 decade five more were created; another was launched in 1938. Then in the 1940 and 1950 decades a spectacular upsurge of these efforts of scientists and generous citizens added about twenty-five more national associations against specific diseases.

Today there are about forty such nationally recognized associations, each supported by the private generosity of individuals, receiving $230 million (in 1964) for their research and other programs.

POLIO

The one new assault launched in the depression was mounted against polio, the dread disease which had nearly ended the promising career of the late President Franklin D. Roosevelt in the 1920s. His friends created the National Foundation and raised great annual sums to fight polio as a tribute to President Roosevelt. These friends supported costly researches which resulted in the discovery of the two vaccines named for their researchers, Dr. Salk and Dr. Sabin. Polio has been almost conquered—last year there were only 121 cases reported in the United States.

The three largest national associations which are fighting named diseases are: The American Cancer Society which received $45 million in 1964; The American Heart Association which received $31 million in 1964, and The National Tuberculosis Association which received $30 million in 1964.

THE NATIONAL HEALTH INSTITUTES

Private generosity financed much of the early medical research that has made exciting assaults on long-dreaded diseases during this century.

Its successes also stimulated the federal government to vastly expanded appropriations for medical research. The public response to the urgent appeals of private philanthropy for funds to finance determined efforts to reduce the deadly effects of diseases proved to the Congress that the people approved of medical research. As a consequence, undreamed-of amounts are provided by the federal government to the National Health Institutes for allocation to medical research in hundreds of laboratories and clinics. Here again is a striking illustration of private generosity pioneering a great public service and also stimulating the interest of the citizens so that legislators sense the public desire for governmental action.

1964 REPORT ON MEDICAL RESEARCH

A recent report, entitled "Facts on the Major Killing and Crippling Diseases in the United States Today," published by the National Health Education Committee states:

> That $1.5 billion is being spent on medical research by the government, the pharmaceutical industry and the major voluntary health organizations.

Further cited are these reductions in death rates since 1944 as a result of research:

> Polio has been eliminated as a fatal disease; the death rate from tuberculosis is down by 87 percent; appendicitis 85 percent; syphilis 36 percent; and influenza 88 percent.
> Despite this record, many diseases still are major killers. At the head of the list is cardiovascular disease, which in 1962 caused 55 percent of all the deaths in the United States. The second leading killer is cancer, which caused 16 percent of all deaths.

XII

TWO SOCIAL CHALLENGES
TO PRIVATE GENEROSITY

The private generosity of Americans pioneered the attack on a social need—old age pensions—over a period of more than two centuries, before the voters and legislators of our nation were ready to meet the need by government action.

In addition, private generosity and initiative of Americans pioneered another attack on a still greater social need—the emancipation of slaves—but failed to bring the nation to a peaceful solution of that problem.

OLD AGE PENSIONS

The challenge was a growing need and demand for non-pauperizing provisions for retirement pay and old age pensions for persons who could not, or did not, lay aside funds to support themselves after their productive years. This desire was not new in America in the twentieth century, but the widespread unemployment and the economic collapse of the 1930s brought millions to the end of their reserves—the need was acute and the demand became insistent.

Fortunately, philanthropists had been busily working on this social need for two centuries. In 1717 the Presbyterian General

Assembly had created a system of pensions for its retired ministers and their widows and had given it a quaint name, such as only Philadelphians could produce, "The Fund for Pious Uses." In due time the more modern name, The Presbyterian Board of Pensions, replaced the original title. For over 200 years it received gifts and grants and offerings, and allocated relief and pensions to the extent of its resources.

Then, in 1926, the General Assembly appointed a laymen's committee of which the Honorable Will H. Hays was chairman and the Honorable Andrew W. Mellon was treasurer. This committee raised $15 million by subscription from members of the churches; and an actuarily planned, contributory system of automatic pensions was created, making a Presbyterian minister's retirement pay a pension which his own premiums had helped to provide—it was no longer a charitable handout.

Other Christian denominations were acting in the same way. Under the leadership of Bishop William Lawrence, the Episcopal Church set up a contributory pension system for its clergy. Through the generosity of John D. Rockefeller, the Baptist Church put a similar plan into effect.

In the field of education, Andrew Carnegie began grants in 1905, which totaled many millions of dollars, to establish a contributory system of pensions for college teachers. The system was called the Teachers' Insurance and Annuity Association— it brought thousands of members of college faculties under its coverage.

Labor and corporations took up the idea. Great corporations, one after the other, recognized their responsibilities to provide pensions for employees who had given lives of service; and a great many corporations set up retirement pension systems, some contributory, some of other characteristics.

By the 1930 decade there was a wide pension coverage of millions of people, but there were other millions who did not enjoy the coverage. As a result, the Roosevelt administration undertook to get Congressional approval for a universal coverage of Social Security benefits for all employed persons. A

Social Security Act was passed and put into operation in his second term of office.

The relatively small program of "The Fund for Pious Uses," set up for Presbyterian Ministers 225 years earlier, had set the pace for a comprehensive coverage with old age benefits for practically every family in the nation.

Tragically, not one kind word for the little band of preachers in Philadelphia, who had planted the mustard seed in 1717 from which this tree had grown, was ever expressed. On the contrary, at the Democratic Convention of 1952, huge gloating banners were unfurled to tell the achievements of the Roosevelt years. On one banner was the word "Charity." It had been crossed out and the words "Social Security" had been written in its place.

Private generosity for the public good does its pioneering and rejoices when the voters sense the worth of its plan and adopt it into the tax-supported family. Sometimes someone remembers to thank the original generous men and women for their pioneering vision and generosity; but *more often* the populace, who ultimately benefit personally from the generous pioneers, do not thank them. They probably do not have even a notion as to how the social reform was originally set in motion.

THE EMANCIPATION OF SLAVES

The other social challenge to private generosity lost:

> For all sad words of tongue or pen
> The saddest of these:
> "It might have been!" (Whittier, in "Maude Muller")

For eighty-five years—1775-1860—private citizens endeavored to abolish slavery in the United States and might have succeeded on the merits of that great moral issue alone, had not politicians exploited the states rights issue to incite rebellion.

The framers of the Constitution had tried, in 1787, to provide for emancipation in that document, but were prevented by the threats of South Carolina and Georgia to withdraw. At any rate, private generosity made a valiant try.

It was in Philadelphia that they began their fight. The Quakers of that city had made strong protests against slavery as early as 1696. In 1774 the Friends excluded from membership in their society all persons who engaged in the slave traffic or who would not free their own slaves.

In 1775 they organized an Anti-Slavery Society. Of course its real name was much more Philadelphian—"The Pennsylvania Society for Promoting the Abolition of Slavery, the Relief of Free Negroes Unlawfully Held in Bondage, and for Improving the Condition of the African Race." It was headed by James Pemberton and Dr. Benjamin Rush. After the Revolutionary War it was reorganized under Benjamin Franklin— as president! It began an enlarged program, and by 1825 there were said to be 140 abolition societies in the United States, 106 of which were in the South.

The phrase "Drumfire of Exhortation"[1] has been used to describe the public appeals which were made in England in the late fifteenth and sixteenth centuries for cooperation in repairing the social structure of that nation. A comparable "drumfire" rolled out of pulpits, hustings, journals and books in the North against human slavery during the second quarter of the nineteenth century.

England had abolished slave trading in 1811 and slavery, itself, in 1833. Denmark and France had also abolished it, and the whole concept was in disgrace throughout the civilized world. General Washington had freed his own slaves in his will, and many other citizens of the South were unhappy about slavery.

Harriet Beecher Stowe's *Uncle Tom's Cabin* (1852) stirred a moral fervor against slavery. The best spirit of America spoke

---

[1] W. K. Jordan, *Philanthropy, op. cit.*

out loudly against the inhumane practice. Henry Ward Beecher held a mock public auction of a white "slave" girl in his Plymouth Church in Brooklyn. Benjamin Lundy, William Lloyd Garrison, Elijah Lovejoy, Wendell Phillips, Charles Sumner, William E. Channing, Bryant, Longfellow, Whittier, Whitman—all thundered by voice or pen against this disgrace to America.

But some shots were fired on the flag at Fort Sumter, South Carolina—and public indignation lost to political hotheads! Lincoln called for troops, and bloody warfare had to finish what private initiative had started so well.

The problem of justice for the Negro race still confronts America. The Civil War was not the only event which frustrated the people of goodwill from giving the blessings of full citizenship to Negroes.

There was a magnificent outburst of philanthropic activity immediately after the war in their behalf. The Peabody Fund, the Slater Fund, John D. Rockefeller, Sr., George Eastman, Julius Rosenwald and a dozen of the Christian denominations gave scores of millions of dollars and deep personal commitment to establishing education for the Negroes after their emancipation.

The first Ku Klux Klan plague swept across the South and infected these efforts with poisonous hate and violence.

After World War I a Southern Methodist Minister, the Reverend Will W. Alexander, launched a plan for group discussions between black and white leaders about mutual community interests in many states and cities of the South. But the second Ku Klux Klan plague swept over the land. It was less effective than the first for the leaders whom we chanced to meet were far more interested in collecting the membership dues than in ideological exploitation. Just the same, they hampered Alexander's Commission on Interracial Cooperation, which would have mitigated—and might even have prevented—the racial bitterness and injustices of the 1960s.

XIII

THE SCOPE OF
AMERICAN GENEROSITY

The 975,000 privately supported agencies can be placed in categories which suggest the nature of their services; and the givers to these causes can be placed in four major categories. Furthermore, the amounts of the gifts which are received by each category of recipient agencies can be documented accurately.

WHAT ARE THE 975,000 AGENCIES WHICH ARE
SUPPORTED BY PRIVATE GENEROSITY?

These agencies are national, state, local and neighborhood in scope and service. For illustration, the National Tuberculosis Association was inaugurated sixty years ago as a non-profit movement to fight tuberculosis. It has waged a winning battle with funds given by generous people and with the proceeds from the sale of its annual Christmas seals; it has established 2,162 state and local associations, through which thousands of volunteers serve each year in a determined assault on this disease. Each of these local associations is a unit in the total scope of private generosity. So it is with forty other "disease" agencies, such as cancer, heart, polio, arthritis and others.

Agencies which have been created to nurture the character and ideals of youth, such as Boy Scouts, Girl Scouts and a score of others, also have thousands of local units, manned by volunteers who supervise the recreational and character-building programs for millions of youths.

These local units are an essential part of America's total private generosity. And so is each local chapter or committee or branch of hundreds of national and state cultural, relief, religious, educational, welfare and service societies and councils and commissions in the United States. These outposts are supported by private generosity and manned by volunteers. It is all these national, state, county, local and neighborhood organized agencies which total 975,000.

The following is an estimate of the scope of the American "epidemic of private generosity" for the public good.

The author is fully aware that this estimate may fail to mention by name some extremely important groups of agencies which deserve mention.

Risk of such omissions seems inevitable, when one attempts to give only a brief overall glimpse of the vast extent and endless variety of private generosity for the public good in America.

Fortunately, an interested reader can assemble listings and catalogues of these hundreds of thousands of agencies from other sources.

American Agencies for the Public Good
Which Are Supported by Private Generosity

		National, Regional, State, Local Units
1.	*Religious*	353,637
2.	*Health*	86,324
3.	*Education*	87,437
4.	*Youth-Recreation and Character Building*	323,368
5.	*General Welfare and Relief*	63,989
6.	*Cultural, Service and Inter-Group*	45,795
7.	*Private Foundations*	15,000
	Total	975,550

The nature of the various institutions, societies and activities which make up these seven large categories of agencies supported by private generosity is obvious in the following:

	National, Regional, State and Local Units
1. *Religious*	
Churches of all faiths	320,000
National Councils of Catholic women, Catholic men, Jewish women, and Protestant women	23,637
Other units of service	10,000
Total	353,637
2. *Health*	
Private Hospitals	6,923
American Red Cross	3,555
American Hospital Auxiliaries	3,527
40 associations to combat named diseases and afflictions	72,319
Total	86,324
3. *Education*	
Independent colleges	1,312
Independent schools	4,100
Non-public schools (elementary, 13,574; secondary 4,061)	17,635
National Education Association	6,514
Public libraries	7,500
American Association of University Women	1,476
P. T. A.'s	45,200
Museums and art galleries	3,200
Other educational and cultural societies and agencies	500
Total	87,437

4. *Youth-Recreation and Character Building*

Boy Scouts	135,000
Girl Scouts	163,000
Boys Clubs, Girls Clubs, Big Brothers, C.Y.O.s, Camp Fire Girls, Settlement Houses, etc.	4,000
Y. M. & Y. W. C. A., Y. M. & Y. W. H. A., Jewish Community Centers, U. S. O.	10,000
Summer camps (welfare and youth)	7,368
Others	4,000
Total	323,368

5. *General Welfare and Relief*   63,989

It is about as difficult to catalogue and count the myriads of agencies in the manifestation of private generosity in the United States for the needy, the poor, the jobless and the homeless as it would be to count the flakes in a snow storm. For example, the National Association of Social Workers publishes a *Social Work Year Book* every five years in which they list the well-organized agencies of welfare and relief—it requires eighty pages to list and describe briefly voluntary national agencies, a great many of which are in the fields of welfare and relief. Some of these national agencies have hundreds, even thousands, of local units of service. Included in this listing are the National Catholic Welfare Conference, the United Jewish Appeal and the United Community Funds and Councils.

The estimated number, above, of all national, regional, state and local units of service in this category of private generosity for the public good is extremely conservative.

6. *Cultural, Service and Inter-Group*

General Federation of Women's Clubs	15,000
Association of Junior Leagues of America	184
American Association for the United Nations	238
National Association for the Advancement of Colored People	1,491

National Conference of Christians & Jews	364
National Council of Negro Women	118
National Federation of Business and Professional Women	3,400
Garden and Horticultural Clubs; Musical and Choral Societies; Historical and Genealogical Societies; Racial and National Origin Societies; Wildlife, Conservation, Recreation Societies (Isaac Walton League); Planned Parenthood Foundation of America; Poetry Society and Societies for many other Arts; Patriotic Societies; Research and Scientific Societies; Community Improvements, including firehouses, playgrounds, rescue squads, vacation day schools, etc.;	
Miscellaneous	25,000
Total	45,795

7. *Private Foundations*   15,000

The American foundations are not unique in their nature, but they are unique in their number and scope and administrative skill.

Foundations or endowments of considerable size were set up around the Christian Church and its institutions in the fourth century and in the following centuries. Dr. Frederick P. Keppel, late distinguished president of The Carnegie Corporation, wrote ". . . From the fourth century until the Reformation, practically all endowments were church endowments." By the same token, hundreds of foundations existed in England in the fifteenth and sixteenth centuries. Most of these were relatively small, but had many of the basic characteristics of the modern American foundations.

In America, Peabody, Rosenwald, Carnegie, Rockefeller, Ford, Mellon and other generous men of the late nineteenth and early twentieth centuries launched a new era for private generosity through the great foundations they created and the intelligent administrations which they provided for the wise application of their funds. In 1964 there were about 15,000 American foundations.[1]

Who gives the over $10 billion per year?

(Following are figures for 1963 from
Giving U. S. A. published by The American
Association of Fund-Raising Counsel)

Individuals gave	$ 7,875,000,000
Foundations gave	819,000,000
Business Corporations gave	536,000,000
Charitable Bequests	795,000,000
Total for 1963	$10,025,000,000

Which agencies receive the gifts of over $10 billion?

(Following are figures for 1963 from
Giving U. S. A. published by The American
Association of Fund-Raising Counsel)

Religion	$ 4,912,250,000
Education	1,704,250,000
Health	1,203,000,000
Welfare	1,503,750,000
Foundations (paid into)	401,000,000
Other (including civic and cultural)	300,750,000
	$10,025,000,000

(Note: Gifts for Youth Agencies are included in the above totals
for Religion, Education and Other)

---

[1] *The Foundation Directory*, Ann D. Walton and Marianna O. Lewis, eds. (New York: Foundation Library Center, F. Emerson Andrews, Director, 1964).

XIV

PERSONAL EXPERIENCES

WITH AMERICAN GENEROSITY

The publishers of this book have requested the author to add this chapter to the original manuscript in order to identify himself and his career actively with the subject and contents of the book. Apparently, the publisher feels that some readers would like to know what aroused the author's interest in this unique subject of private generosity for the public good, and by what experiences he acquired a knowledge of it.

PERSONAL EXPERIENCES OF THE AUTHOR WITH GENEROUS AMERICANS

For forty years I have been a partner in a firm which has counseled several thousand non-profit educational, religious, health and welfare institutions in regard to finances. Those which we have counseled have received between $2 billion and $3 billion in gifts and bequests from generous men and women.

The profession of counseling philanthropic institutions is less than a half century old, and I have been asked—many times—how I happened to enter it. As a matter of fact, I didn't enter it—there was no such profession to enter when I was ready to start a career.

Through a set of unplanned circumstances I found myself one of a dozen or so men, some of us not even known to each other, who were unknowingly creating a new service profession in the first quarter of the twentieth century in the United States.

My first job after graduation from Oberlin College in 1910 was on the staff of Lyman L. Pierce, who was then general secretary of the Pittsburgh, Pennsylvania, Y. M. C. A., where I was secretary for boys' work.

Lyman Pierce had just returned from a two-year duty in Australia and New Zealand, where he had helped the Y. M. C. A. of those two British nations raise funds for modern Y. M. C. A. plants in their leading cities. He was at his best in stirring the Christian leaders of a great city to action and generosity in providing well-equipped Y. M. C. A. buildings for strengthening the moral and spiritual characters of their youth. He proceeded to build a half dozen new Y. M. C. A. buildings in populous sections of metropolitan Pittsburgh. I was a young green member of Pierce's staff. I was caught up in his bold plans, and thus was unconsciously helping to create the new profession of fund-raising counseling for philanthropic institutions. Actually, I was launching myself on a career unlike anything I had ever dreamed, because at that time no such career had been dreamed of by anyone!

TWO YOUNG MEN DISCOVERED NEW WAYS TO STIMULATE GENEROSITY

This new service profession, which a few of us were creating, grew out of a base laid by Lyman L. Pierce and Charles S. Ward.

Both of these men were young secretaries in the Young Men's Christian Association. Lyman L. Pierce, after graduating from the University of Minnesota in 1892, went into Y. M. C. A. work, where an early job led him to become the financial and membership secretary in Omaha, Nebraska. Being a young man of superior ideals, spiritual capabilities and courageous initiative, he was disturbed because his time was being devoted almost entirely to financial efforts necessary to keep the work alive. Far from accepting the situation, he began to work out a plan by which he could compress his membership and fund-raising tasks into a brief space of time and thus free himself during the remainder of the year for character-building work among the young men of the community.

Pierce enlisted 100 of the leading men of Omaha in a Y. M. C. A. membership campaign—each man to get one new member a month, until the total membership would reach 1,500. Teams were set up (twenty teams); printed matter was prepared; and regular report meetings held. It was a great success—and lots of fun as well. News of the new method spread quickly throughout the entire Y. M. C. A.

Charles S. Ward entered the employ of the Y. M. C. A. when he was graduated from Dartmouth in 1881. In 1890 he became general secretary at Grand Rapids, Michigan, where he persuaded his directors to agree to close down their desks for a month and see a set number of people each day for subscriptions for the work of the Y. M. C. A., promising that if they would do this, nothing more would need to be said or done about finances the rest of the year.

The newspapers told of this novel undertaking—"spectacular" it was termed in those days—and the whole city watched with intense interest. The eleven-month recess from financial solicitation proved a happy experience. It also proved so interesting to the rest of the Y. M. C. A. brotherhood that Ward was called in 1897 to New York as financial secretary of the International Committee of the Y. M. C. A. City after city invited Ward to tell other local associations of his experience at Grand Rapids and to help them put similar campaigns into operation.

Meanwhile, in 1900, Lyman Pierce had been appointed to the general secretaryship of the Y. M. C. A. in Washington, D. C. With his restless energy he brought about an extension of the program and gradually persuaded his directors to undertake to erect a new building to cost the unprecedented sum of $300,000, receiving a strong backing from President Theodore Roosevelt. In 1905 Pierce requested the International Committee for the help of Ward in directing the $300,000 campaign in Washington—and, here the paths of the two men met. Merging their ideas and experiences, they evolved the modern "whirlwind" campaign. It was Pierce who made the bold suggestion that the campaign be cut down from a month's to a week's time and that, in order to accomplish this result, a larger number of volunteer solicitors be enlisted. It worked!

The Pierce-Ward Procedure

Following the Washington experience, Ward adopted the "one week" plan as his standard practice. From that time on he directed similar Y. M. C. A. building campaigns in scores of cities. So widespread were his campaigns that they came to be known as the "Ward" plan. The greatest of these early efforts occurred in New York City in 1913, when the Y. M. C. A. and the Y. W. C. A. jointly determined to raise $4 million for needed new buildings. This announcement took New York's breath away, because no single event in the field of philanthropy had ever been of so spectacular a nature as the unbelievable proposal to raise $4 million in a few days. But the campaign was a success. A total of $4,095,000 was contributed by 17,400 people; and 400 of the contributors—including the John D. Rockefellers, father and son—gave $3,500,-000 in large amounts, while 17,000 others followed their lead with smaller contributions totaling $495,000.

This and other similar achievements of the campaign method now began to attract the attention of hospitals, colleges and various welfare societies. Charles Ward was in great demand, and almost everywhere he went an amazing success resulted.

Lyman Pierce later spent a year traveling across the United States as field secretary of the Layman's Missionary Movement, and gave instruction and inspiration in the new technique of raising philanthropic funds to laymen in the Protestant churches. The intensive campaign method was adopted by many churches in what was called the Every-Member Canvass; and, as a consequence, giving to Protestant churches experienced a sharp rise, which has continued to this day.

Just prior to America's entry into World War I, President Woodrow Wilson appointed Henry P. Davison, a J. P. Morgan partner, president of the American Red Cross and requested him to raise a $100 million fund for the war-time use of the Red Cross. Since this was a stunning undertaking, the largest appeal to American generosity ever projected up to that time, Davison called upon Charles Ward to counsel him in the use of the new magical fund-raising campaign techniques. Ward enlisted Pierce as his associate, and the two creators of this new fund-raising method were brought into national view.

Following this spectacular success, and after the war was over, other philanthropies came to Ward and Pierce to learn how to raise great funds so quickly. As a consequence, Ward and Pierce organized a firm of fund-raising counselors in 1919, and were kind enough to invite me to become a partner.[1] In 1926 George E. Lundy—general secretary of the Y. M. C. A. of Canton, Ohio—and I organized our own firm, and in 1932 Dr. Louis W. Robey, a lawyer in Philadelphia, joined us as a partner and officer. Within the next several years, fifty other able men became associated with our firm.

It has been a rare privilege to spend a life in active association with thousands of dedicated people in America who devote much of the "overflow" of their lives in helpful service to others. This has been my privilege for over four decades in the midst of the fabulous twentieth century. I have seen these people stand at the edge of human suffering and extend the hand of rescue to a despairing mother, a hungry child, a jobless father. I have seen others go from office to office, from

---

[1] See Armand C. Marts, *Man's Concern for His Fellow Man* (New York: Marts & Lundy, Inc., 1961).

home to home, to sound a rally for a hospital, a youth club, a library. I have been present time and again when men and women, tired from their day's work, spent six long evening hours in raising funds for an educational addition to their church in order that the teen-agers of the community might receive religious and spiritual training.

My associates and I have counseled over the years about 4,000,000 volunteer workers of that sort, all giving their overflow energies for the good of others without earthly compensation. They were paid only in the coin of that spiritual realm where "neither moth nor rust doth corrupt and where thieves do not break through and steal."

In my associations with these unselfish persons, I have often felt that I was standing at the very cutting edge of civilization itself, where a noble culture was being shaped by people who really cared.

We helped to build over 1,200 recitation halls, libraries, laboratories, dormitories, chapels, student centers, gymnasiums, etc. on the campuses of over 400 colleges, seminaries and schools. We helped to add hundreds of millions of dollars to educational and cultural endowments.

We helped to build and support hundreds of hospitals, scout troops, character-building youth agencies, Christian and Jewish centers, settlement houses, orphanages, old folks homes and welfare services.

We helped to build 1,000 churches and religious edifices.

We helped to add nearly $2 billion to the resources of 12,-000 of America's finest institutions of religion, education, health, culture and character.

Is it any wonder that I regard as a rare privilege my associations with the unselfish Americans who give their talent, time and money to the accomplishment of these additions to the American culture?

The publishers of this book have also requested that I tell of some of the personalities, events and experiences encountered in this career. Perhaps, the following will be of interest.

Visitors from the Ozarks

Dr. Lynn Wylie Hurie was a dedicated young minister who left his comfortable post as an assistant pastor of the Brick Presbyterian Church, when it stood on Fifth Avenue in New York, and accepted the presidency of a small struggling college in Arkansas, the College of the Ozarks. When I asked him why, he replied, "Because no one else would, and 400 ambitious boys and girls must not be turned away."

Having accepted the challenge, Dr. Hurie was making progress when a fire destroyed the college gymnasium. In obvious need, he came to me in New York for counsel. I asked, "Do the students know of your mission to New York?" He said, "The whole student body gathered at the station to see me off, just as though I were the football team; they're waiting for daily bulletins from me." I asked, "Would one or two of those students come to New York to help you look for generous donors?" A few days later he reported that the entire student body had subscribed a travel fund for two seniors, a boy and a girl, to come to New York to help him.

The New York papers published the news story and sent their reporters to meet the two students upon their arrival at the station. Generous men and women were invited to luncheons and teas to meet Dr. Hurie and his two students. Two generous ladies, one in New York and the other in New Jersey, among others, became deeply interested and during the subsequent years made gifts to the College of the Ozarks which exceeded many thousand-fold the cost of the trip to New York, financed by the Ozark College boys and girls.

Dr. Henry Sloane Coffin Emptied His Checking Account

One of the luncheons for Dr. Hurie was assembled at the Union League Club by Dr. Henry Sloane Coffin, late president of Union Theological Seminary, of which Dr. Hurie was a graduate. After the luncheon, Dr. Coffin returned to his office, and requested his secretary to write a check to the College of the Ozarks for whatever balance there might be in his checking account.

A Surprise Gift

This episode brings to mind the story of a surprising gift made at another luncheon at the Union League Club. That occasion was in support of the Salvation Army's plan to build a guest house for itinerant men. It would cost about $200,000, as I recall the story, and they needed the last $75,000 to complete the fund—and it was proving hard to come by. A score of generous businessmen were invited to a luncheon at the Union League Club to discuss the matter. The meal was over, and the chairman was on his feet presenting the problem when the door suddenly opened and in burst a late invitee, who interrupted with an apology for his unavoidable delay saying he must be excused within eight minutes for another appointment. He asked for a fast briefing. The chairman responded promptly, closing with the statement that it was necessary for the Salvation Army to raise the final $75,000 at once. The newcomer thanked the chairman, looked at his watch and said, "I will be glad to send you the $75,000. Now, if you will kindly excuse me, I must go on." And so he did, leaving the other gentlemen nothing else to do but adjourn, *sine die*.

A 25-cent Gift to a Panhandler Saved the Giver's Life

William M. Kingsley—late president of the United States Trust Company of New York City and an active leader in many community, philanthropic, religious and character-building agencies—always found it difficult to turn aside a street beggar even though appearances might make it seem that he was a professional panhandler. Kingsley's Wall Street associates laughingly called him a "soft touch" and chided him about being a street beggar's "angel." Kingsley laughed at this characterization and told me an amazing story of how his life was saved one day in Wall Street when he stopped to give a beggar a quarter. This was his story:

It happened on September 16, 1920, when someone, probably an anarchist, exploded a bomb against the front of the office of J. P. Morgan Co. on Wall Street, killing thirty people, injuring a hundred more and causing millions of dollars of damage.

Kingsley who had a luncheon date on Exchange Place at 12:15 P. M. on that day, stepped out of his bank on Wall Street at noon to start a short walk, past the J. P. Morgan office at the corner of Wall and Exchange, around to the place of his luncheon on Exchange Place. As he stepped off the steps of the U. S. Trust Company a beggar stopped him and asked for a handout. Kingsley paused, reached into his pocket, pulled out some change and handed the beggar a quarter; and at that very moment, up the street and a few yards away, the bomb exploded at the very point which he would have been passing had not the beggar delayed him!

When I asked Mr. Kingsley if this was a lesson in generosity, charity, compassion, he said it had no philosophical moral—it was just a happenstance. "But the fact was," said he, "giving the quarter saved my life." And he added, "My friends were much less vocal subsequently in criticizing me as a 'soft touch' for a street beggar."

The Southern Methodist Centenary Program in 1919

Promptly after the close of World War I, the churches of all faiths in the United States projected post-war rehabilitation and expanded missionary programs which called for contributions of funds in previously unheard of amounts for religious purposes. The success of Henry P. Davison's Red Cross campaign for $100 million and the subsequent United Wartime Service Campaign for the various wartime agencies for $170 million had initiated an entirely new era in generosity and philanthropy amongst the American people. All non-profit agencies stepped up their programs and their financial budgets; and the religious forces of the nation joined in this upsurge. The Southern Methodist Church was then a separate organization from the Northern Methodist Church with its headquarters at Nashville, Tennessee.

The Southern Methodist Church leaders invited me to go to Nashville to counsel them on raising a $35 million fund for their post-war missionary and expansion program. An organization was promptly and energetically set up throughout the southern states where the Southern Methodist Churches were located. Within a period of six months, a fund of over $50 million was subscribed, representing a spectacular breakthrough for their church and for that section of the nation. There was much discussion, indeed some gossip, among the 2,000,000 members of the churches as to how it was accomplished. The gossip was about an enormous fee which must have been paid to a fund-raising counselor from New York City for his services in the program. I was that person. Someone had started a rumor that I had been paid a 6 percent commission. This, of course, was laughable for I had been paid a monthly salary of $2,000 out of which I had paid my own living expenses while at Nashville.

When the gossip spread throughout the South in a harmful manner, the leaders of the Southern Methodist Church called me on the phone and asked how they could counteract the untruthful rumors. My reply was, "Why don't you just tell them the truth—that my whole compensation for the six months period was $2,000 a month, out of which I paid my own hotel and living expenses in Nashville." Certainly, there was quite a gap between $2,000 a month for six months, my actual fee, and 6 percent of $50 million, which would have been $3 million. The difference would amount to $2,988,000. That is a pretty good measuring rod for much of the ill-founded rumor in the misunderstood field of compensation for ethical fund-raising counselors.

The Theodore Roosevelt Memorial Association

When former President Theodore Roosevelt died unexpectedly of a stroke, in January, 1919, his death was a great shock to the American people and a severe blow to the plans of the Republican Party, because the Republicans were hoping to regain control of the government via the 1920 election and had persuaded Roosevelt to become the candidate for president of the reunited party in that year.

A few days after his death, I received a telephone call from New York while I was in Nashville (counseling on the $35 million program referred to above for the Southern Methodist Church). My New York caller told me that he and others had formed a Theodore Roosevelt Memorial Association, that they wanted me to counsel them in raising the funds which would be needed and that they planned an appeal for funds in connection with the celebration in October of Roosevelt's birthday.

I agreed to assist. The officers and directors of the Roosevelt Memorial Association with whom I worked the next several months included several of the outstanding statesmen and businessmen of that era: Senator Elihu Root, who had been Secretary of War in Roosevelt's cabinet; former Governor and later Chief Justice Charles Evans Hughes; Honorable Will H. Hays; George W. Perkins, partner in J. P. Morgan & Co.; General George W. Goethals, builder of the Panama Canal; Colonel William Boyce Thompson; Colonel T. Coleman du Pont; General Leonard Wood.

Many suggestions were offered as to the nature of the memorial. Some, of course, proposed spectacular monuments in the city of Washington. The members of Roosevelt's family, however, expressed serious doubt as to the propriety of an immediate decision concerning any massive memorial at the national capital, because they felt that it would be better for a future generation to create such a memorial in the light of a longer range historical view. Consequently, the 1919 Roosevelt Memorial Association's plans included the purchase of Roosevelt's birthplace on Twenty-second Street in New York City and its maintenance as a national memorial, and the establishment of an endowed fund which would honor three men each year with citations for their public services in the spirit of Roosevelt's own career. A few million dollars were quickly and generously offered by the American people in the fall of 1919 for these purposes.

The Shorter Catechism Earned $100,000 for a College

The president of a little college in Dakota visited me one day with anxiety in his heart and on his face. He wanted much more money for his college and had come to New York in the hope of finding some generous contributors. I knew of a Scotsman who had made a large fortune in this country and who had a warm sympathy for ambitious boys and girls who wanted to go to college but found it financially difficult to pay their way; so I told him about this man and he set out to visit him.

The following week he dropped in again and reported that he had had a very pleasant visit with the Scotsman, but had not come away with any money. He reported his interview about like this:

The Scotsman: "Have you taught all the students in your college to recite the shorter catechism?"

College president: "No."

Scotsman: "When you teach them the shorter catechism, come back and tell me and I will help you."

A year later the college president went back to the Scotsman and reported that every boy and girl at his college could recite the shorter catechism. He was given a check made out to the college for $100,000.

A Case of Buck Fever

A few years ago we were counseling a preparatory school which wished to raise a fund for some new buildings but soon discovered that the headmaster, the chairman of the board and the treasurer did not have the courage or the conviction to ask friends to subscribe to the much-needed fund. There was one very generous couple whose children and grandchildren had attended the school, and the three generations of the family

Marble Collegiate Church, New York. The Collegiate Church, founded in 1628, is the oldest church in America having a continuous ministry.

Lyman L. Pierce—co-creator of the modern fund-raising campaigns.

Will H. Hays—late Postmaster General "czar" of Hollywood.

President Theodore Roosevelt.

President Eisenhower at Transylvania College. (*left*, Senator John Sherman Cooper—*right*, President Frank A. Rose.)

At convocation of the Case Institute of Technology, Cleveland, President Herbert Hoover accepts a citation from Dr. T. Keith Glennan, president.

Louis W. Robey—honorary Vice-Chairman of the Board, Marts & Lundy, Inc.

George E. Lundy—honorary Chairman of the Board, Marts & Lundy, Inc.

The Negro colleges of America express their gratitude to the John D. Rockefeller family for their generosity of three generations. *From left to right,* Dr. Frederick D. Patterson, president of the United Negro Fund; President Dwight Eisenhower; and John D. Rockefeller III.

Winston Churchill at the mid-century convocation of M.I.T., Boston.

had a great affection for the school. They had ample funds and were generous to many philanthropic causes—in fact, the head of the family, whom I knew personally, kept a separate checkbook for his contributions. He religiously gave away each year the Biblical tithe or 10 percent of his income, and would deposit this 10 percent in his special contribution checking account, to be paid out to religious and educational institutions.

In spite of these favorable factors the school officials found excuse after excuse for not asking this generous friend to make a contribution to the fund for the new building. After all my urgings had been turned aside, I proposed to the treasurer that he drive over to see this generous friend whose business was located about ten miles away, offering to go with him in the interview to make it easier for him. He finally accepted my offer, with apparent grim distaste.

We drove to the factory of the businessman, pulling the car up to the rear of his office where there was a vacant parking space. As I stepped out of the car I found myself just outside his first floor office, and he was sitting at his desk by the window. I waved to him. He waved back. I walked to the door, held the door open for the treasurer and waited a moment for him to come alongside of me. He did not come, so I looked back and saw him sitting in the car, frozen to the wheel! Of course, it was too late for me to beat a retreat, so I went in alone and greeted the gentleman we had come to see. He greeted me and asked me to be seated. Briefly, I told him the purpose of the call. Suspecting it, he was ready for us. Immediately, he sent for his secretary and asked, "What balance do I have in my special contributions checkbook?" She told him. He directed her, "Write a check for $10,000 to the order of the school." He signed it and handed it to me. I thanked him warmly and, after a few moments, went back to the auto where the treasurer was sitting, his hands still on the steering wheel. We started back without a word either by him or by me. When we arrived at the school, I reached into my pocket and handed him the check for $10,000. Nothing further was ever said in my presence, either by him or by me. It was a case of "buck fever," I presume.

A College President Was Unable to Speak

The preceding story is not unlike an experience I had with two friends, one of them the late president of a college in Ohio and the other the late A. C. Ernst, founder and head of the great C.P.A. firm of Ernst & Ernst. Ernst was chairman of a college campaign for about $1 million, and one of its trustees.

The president of the college knew it was time in the campaign for him to solicit Ernst's own subscription and the subscriptions of other trustees, but he was busy and also dreaded having to approach his trustees personally for their subscriptions. He asked me for my comments as to how he might do it gracefully and effectively, and as we were discussing this, he broke in with the request that I should go with him and help him in an interview with Ernst. I agreed. He called Ernst in his Cleveland office and made an appointment. We visited him.

We had a pleasant visit with Ernst for nearly a half hour, during which time we talked about the Cleveland Indians, the political situation and other subjects that kept safely away from the solicitation of money. Finally, it was Ernst, himself, who looked at his watch and said, "I'm sorry, but I have an engagement out of the office in about five minutes. Is there anything special you wish to say to me?" At this moment the president turned to me with an appealing look on his face and at a loss as to how to introduce the subject; so I broke in and said, "We believe it would be helpful at this stage of the fund-raising program to ask you and the other trustees of the college if you are ready to make your own subscription." Ernst replied, "I think that is a very good policy." He said no more. By that time we were all on our feet ready to leave. Ernst again primed the conversation by saying, "Did you have an amount in mind that you thought I might give?" and he looked at the president. The latter's lips moved, but no sound came out. He again looked at me in his appealing way and I said, "Yes, Mr. Ernst. We wondered if you would be willing to subscribe $50,000." Ernst responded, "Just the amount I had in mind. Do you have a card with you?" We handed him a card; he signed it, then handed it to the president and said, "I am sorry I have to hurry away." As the president and I went down the hall, he threw his arms around me and, with tears in his eyes, said, "My boy, my boy." It was a satisfaction and a pleasure to be of service to him, for he was so appreciative—and it was a pleasure, likewise, to have had that visit with A. C. Ernst, who also appreciated my help in getting the interview off the ground.

A College President Used the Wrong Brand of Cigarettes

Transylvania College of Lexington, Kentucky, has the distinction of being the oldest college west of the Alleghenies, being founded during the Revolutionary War in 1780. It is still related to the founding Christian Church (Disciples of Christ). Transylvania had the early support of many Revolutionary and national heroes and educated numerous men who became leaders in all phases of American culture of the past two centuries.

Like many other institutions, however, Transylvania encountered problems as well as successes—problems in the years during and following World War II were especially difficult. Then, in 1951, the Trustees of Transylvania elected to the presidency of the college a young graduate who threw the whole weight of his ability, brains, personality, energy and dedication into strengthening his beloved alma mater.

He was Frank A. Rose, born in Mississippi in 1920 to a Disciple of Christ family. He was graduated from Transylvania in 1942, became a minister of the Christian denomination, taught on the Transylvania faculty, took graduate studies at the University of London and Chicago and was elected president of the college at the age of 31.

Resolved to build Transylvania to new strength and quality, he proceeded to do so with amazing vigor and success, asking us to counsel him. President Dwight D. Eisenhower accepted his invitation to speak at a great Transylvania Convocation in Lexington, which brought renewed courage, faith and vision to the friends of this venerable college.

Rose, who led his trustees and alumni and fellow citizens in a spirited search for needed funds, called upon an officer of a tobacco company. As he started his presentation, he automatically drew a package of cigarettes from his pocket, lighted one and went on with his story about Transylvania.

The tobacco company officer looked quizzically at Dr. Rose's cigarette—it was the brand of a competitor. Dr. Rose flushed. Neither spoke. The tobacco official reached into a drawer of his desk, pulled out a package of cigarettes of his own make. Still, neither man spoke. Dr. Rose crushed his cigarette in the ash tray, selected a cigarette from the pack on the table, lighted it and proceeded with his solicitation for Transylvania College.

The tense pantomime ended on a friendly note; and, in due time, Dr. Rose was rewarded.

EXPERIENCES OF GEORGE E. LUNDY AND DR. LOUIS W. ROBEY WITH GENEROUS AMERICANS

My two long-time associates, George E. Lundy and Dr. Louis W. Robey were asked for their permission to include some of their experiences with generous Americans. They kindly consented. First from George E. Lundy:

H. W. Hoover of the Hoover Vacuum Sweeper

During the time that I was secretary of the Y. M. C. A. in Canton, Ohio—from 1913 to 1923—H. W. Hoover, President of the Hoover Suction Sweeper Company of North Canton, was a member of the board of trustees. He was a high-grade Christian gentleman whom everybody loved and respected.

One day he called and asked if I would come to North Canton to visit him, as he had a problem which he would like to discuss with me.

Hoover said, "Mr. Lundy, I was born just one mile east of this factory and I have lived here all my life. As you know, the Hoover Suction Sweeper Company is a very successful organization and it has been made so by the loyalty of the men and women of this community. I am now growing old and I have begun thinking about how I should distribute my estate when it comes to making my will. I want to do something which will be helpful to the people of this community, for they are the ones who have made my wealth possible and I want to leave some of it to them.

"I have been thinking about leaving, in my will, the money to build a hospital, for we have none here. But I am not quite sure that that's what I want to do, and that's why I asked you to come up to see if you could suggest anything better."

My response was, "I will be glad to try, but I would like a couple of weeks to think it over." He agreed.

About two weeks later he called and asked if I had any suggestion. "I will be up tomorrow to talk it over," I told him.

The next day I said to him, "Mr. Hoover, North Canton is only six miles from Canton and there is a well-paved road between the two cities. There are two fine hospitals in Canton, well-built with the best facilities and high-grade staffs. The people of North Canton are just as close to those two hospitals as most of the people who live in Cleveland are to the hospitals located in that city.

"If you leave money in your will with which to build a hospital, it will be used by the people who could use the facilities of the Canton hospitals just as well. I wonder if you would be serving the people of the community better if you would build a building which could be used by all the people of North Canton all the time?"

He asked me to explain. I suggested that he build a Y. M. C. A. which would serve as a community center.

He thought that over for a short time and then said, "I think that is a good suggestion. How much do you think it would cost?" I estimated that $250,000 would be sufficient. He said, "All right, that's what I'll do."

I then asked Hoover if he had $250,000. He replied with

some heat, "You don't think I'd be talking about it if I didn't have it, do you?"

"Do you have it in cash?" I asked. "Could you pay it out now conveniently?" He nodded.

I asked, "Mr. Hoover why do you want to wait till you die? Why don't you do it now? You would have the pleasure of watching all the people of North Canton use the building."

He then queried, "Would you help me?" I agreed.

"All right, that's exactly what we are going to do." He put the program in motion promptly and announced what he was going to do.

During the construction some leaders tried to figure out how they could repay Hoover. They finally decided to present him with a *We Thank You* book which would include the signatures of all the residents of the little city of North Canton.

Printed in gold on the cover of this book were the words, *We Thank You,* with each of the inside pages headed, *We Thank You.* The pages were ruled for the signatures of the people who lived in the community. Interestingly enough, in that little town of about 2,000 population, there were only four people who refused to sign the book. Where there were small children in the family, the mothers guided their hands, so the children could say they signed it, too.

They prepared pen sketches, which were printed in the upper outside corner of each of the left-hand pages, depicting various events and people in the life of Hoover. The first one was a picture of himself; the second, a picture of his wife; another was a picture of the house in which Hoover was born; another was the little office he used at the time he was mayor of the community; and on a number of the pages were pictures of some of the oldest employees of the concern.

When this material had all been gathered, a committee took it to the printing office and stood beside the press on which the work was done, making certain that only one copy of each page was printed, and as it came off the press the committee took a hammer and broke the plate so that there could never be but one copy of the book.

They did all this, and Hoover never heard of it until it was presented—when the building was dedicated. The whole town was invited, and the unique, attractive book was presented to Hoover, who was overcome. He tried to thank the people, but he couldn't. With tears running down his face, he finally sat down, completely overcome. Later he bought a small iron safe which he placed in his office, and in that safe was just one treasure—"The Book," as he always called it. Visitors coming into his office never departed without his showing "The Book."

When his wife died, I was away Upon my return the following week, I went to see him. Sitting in his office, he said to me, "Mr. Lundy, I am getting old now; I don't have much to do with the management of the Hoover Company anymore. The boys are doing that very well. I come over here to the office and sit during the morning, reading the paper and taking care of my little tasks which might come to my desk, and you know what I do then? I go over to the building and I sit there in the lobby and watch the people using it, and it is the greatest thing I ever had happen in my whole life."

H. W. Hoover has passed on, but the building is still there, and the people use it—and they are still thanking H. W. Hoover for it.

College Buildings Which Came from the Wash Tubs

During Abraham Lincoln's first term in the presidency, Salmon P. Chase, whose home was in Cincinnati, Ohio, was secretary of the treasury. He was at that time interested in the Negro problem and made a gift of $10,000 to Wilberforce College which was established in 1863 by the African Methodist Church.

Some time age I was invited to meet with the president of the college to discuss a fund-raising program. When I arrived at his office I found that the bishop of the African Methodist Episcopal Church was also present.

The college already had four or five buildings. I asked them where they got the money to build those buildings, inquiring particularly about any large gifts which they had received.

The bishop replied, "The only large gift this college has ever had was the $10,000 which Mr. Chase gave back during the first term of President Lincoln."

I said to him, "Bishop, where in the world did you get the rest of the money to build these buildings, because they cost a lot more than $10,000?"

He reached over, put his hand on my knee and said, "Mr. Lundy, the money which built these buildings came from the wash tubs and kitchen sink."

I said, "I don't understand what you mean." His reply was, "The money came in amounts of twenty-five cents, fifty cents, and one dollar from hundreds of Negro Methodist women who earned it as scrub women and nursemaids."

H. H. Timken of the Timken Roller Bearing Company

During World War I, I was asked to take charge of the campaigns for the American Red Cross and the Y. M. C. A. in eastern Ohio. I asked H. H. Timken, President of the Timken Roller Bearing Company to be general chairman, and he accepted. We traveled over this territory for several months, and certain incidents stand out in my mind in connection with our relationship which illustrates how unselfish service to a humanitarian cause can enrich a man's life.

We had arranged a luncheon meeting for the leading industrialists in East Liverpool, Ohio, to get the program started in that city. We had several meetings previous to this one and Timken became enthusiastic over the program. At this meeting in East Liverpool he said, "I am a rich man, a very rich man, and during all these years they have been asking me to be chairman of this or that organization. I always said, 'I won't do it —all you are thinking is that if you get me in I will give more money.' They kept telling me how much I would enjoy being of service to my community, but I didn't believe it. I want to tell you gentlemen that I was wrong—I have never been so happy over anything as I have during this campaign, and you men will have the same experience if you get behind it."

One day we were down in the southeastern corner of the state of Ohio at Woodsfield, where we were to have a meeting in the afternoon. We were sitting in the lobby of the little hotel when a telephone call came for Timken. He was very hard of hearing and asked me to take the call. The call was from the superintendent of the Timken factory in Canton, who said the electric power had gone off and the electric furnaces in their steel mill had frozen. He wanted Timken to come home at once. When I repeated the message to Timken, his reply was as follows: "You tell him just exactly what I am saying—you tell him I am out here in this campaign and I am not coming home until it is over, and if those furnaces are not going when I get back some fellow is going to lose his job."

The Most Generous Gift Was for $5.00

The Y. M. C. A. of Canton, Ohio, was holding its final report meeting in an appeal for $250,000 for a new building. H. H. Timken had given the largest amount, $35,000 of it having been announced publicly, and probably much more unannounced.

At the final meeting which was full of civic enthusiasm, Timken was asked to say a few words. He arose to the plaudits of his fellow citizens, hushed their cheers for him and said, "You praise me because you think I made the most generous gift. I did not. You are mistaken. That man sitting over there," he pointed, "gave the most generous gift. He gave five dollars. But I know what that cost him, because he works for the Timken Company. I know what he earns, and I know the size of his family. I may have made the *largest* gift, but *he* made the *most generous gift*."

Lake Chautauqua

Chautauqua Institution—a high-ranking educational and religious organization which had been established for fifty years —found itself, in 1934, in a precarious financial position. It had debts aggregating $750,000 on which they had not been able to pay interest for the past three or four years and had been thrown into receivership. They called on us to counsel them.

In this institution there were many fine people who applied themselves to the effort of giving and raising the money. However, there were two outstanding persons without whom success would have been impossible. These two were Ralph Norton, President of the Acme Steel Company and Mrs. Thomas A. Edison, whose father was one of the founders of Chautauqua.

Norton had been interested in Chautauqua for many years, was a member of the board of trustees, and had built and given to the institution a very fine building to house their opera and plays. During the debt reducing program he subscribed about $75,000. Three days before the program was to close, we found ourselves in the position of having to raise $105,000 in order to achieve success, and success looked rather dubious. I went to Norton and explained the situation, telling him that without another large gift it was impossible for the campaign to succeed. He asked me what I thought he should do about it, and I suggested he agree to give $35,000 more on the condition that the other $70,000 would be subscribed within the next three days. His reply was, "Mr. Lundy, I think I have done my share." I replied, "I think you have, too, Mr. Norton, but let me tell you a story."

I asked him if he knew of a little, rather run-down cottage located next to a cafeteria and right across the street from the St. Elmo Hotel in which a little old lady lived alone. He said he knew of it, and I then told him, "The little old lady who lives there came to the office a few days ago and said to me, 'Mr. Lundy, I do not have any money and I have no income. I can only live on funds which my friends give me from time to time. I received a check this morning from a friend of mine for five dollars and I want to give this to the campaign to save Chautauqua.' I told her she did not have to make a subscription and she said, 'But I want to—I wish I could make it more, but this is all I can do.' Norton responded, "Well, when you tell me a story like that, I am not sure I have done my share. I would like to talk the matter over with Mrs. Norton. Will you come back this afternoon to see me again?"

In the conference that afternoon he told me that he and Mrs. Norton had agreed to accept the suggestion of giving $35,000 more on the condition that the other $70,000 would be raised by the time the campaign closed, but that he did not care to have any announcement of the subscription made. I told him that would defeat the whole thing and urged him to allow us to make the announcement that he he was making the subscription under that condition. He agreed. The other $70,000 was secured, making the program a success. Needless to say, Mrs. Edison also had a big part in it. The "little lady" sparked the success with her $5.00 gift. The widow's mite was a mighty help for Chautauqua.

"I Dare You"

The fund-raising program for Blessing Hospital in Quincy, Illinois, was going along all right, except that we could not get any cooperation from the employees of the largest industrial plant in the city. Upon inquiry, I found that there was just one man among the employees who was bitterly opposed to the hospital; and he was leader enough to prevent building an organization in the plant for the hospital. I persuaded another man who was interested in the company to ask the opponent to come to the office the following night so that I could discuss it with him. He replied, "I don't think I can get the man to do it." So, I told him, "Tell the man I *dare* him to come to the office."

The following night I was in the office, alone, when a man walked in. He said, "I understand you want to see me." I asked, "Who are you?" He replied, "I am the man you dared to come see you." I countered, "Oh, you are the fellow who is stopping the building of an organization at the plant for the hospital." He hedged, saying he couldn't stop the men; they could go ahead if they wanted to. I asked, "Now, what I want to know is why you are doing it." He willingly answered, "Well, my wife was in the hospital for an operation, and after the operation was over she died." When I asked if the hospital was to blame, or if there was anything they did they should not have done, he said, "Not that I know of." I asked if he thought the doctor was to blame. He said he didn't think so. So I queried, "Then what is the trouble—why are you opposed to this move?" "Well," he said, "after my wife died I went to the telephone and called her sister and then put in another call for the undertaker, and when I got the bill from the hospital they charged me twenty cents for those two telephone calls."

I made no reply, but stood there looking at him and smiled. There was a silence for a couple of minutes. Finally he suggested, "That doesn't sound so darn hot, does it?" I answered "No, that doesn't sound so darn hot." Again there was silence for a minute or so, after which he asked, "Well, what do you want me to do." I responded, "You are the fellow who has prevented the organization; consequently, you are the fellow who can build the organization in your plant, so I am appointing you the chairman in your company to promote this campaign among the employees." What a job he did!

EXPERIENCES OF DR. LOUIS W. ROBEY WITH GENEROUS AMERICANS

An Ambiguous Answer

We were counseling a seminary in a development program. In order to make the needs known, we suggested some meetings in various cities of wealthy laymen. There was considerable resistance to having these meetings of twenty or twenty-five men, who were to be told the needs of the seminary by the president. It was to be hoped that the men would offer generous support for the seminary at a suitable time later on.

At our first meeting the president of the seminary sat next to a man who had large means, but was a very modest person. During the course of the meeting the president approached me and, in a whispered critical conversation said, "I thought you said that all these men were wealthy."

I said, "They are."

He replied, "That man next to me is not."

I looked and asked, "What makes you think that he is not?"

"I asked him what his business is, and he told me he runs a grocery store."

"He not only runs one grocery store," I pointed out, "but he also runs a chain of several hundred stores, one of the biggest grocery chains in the country."

Later, the "grocer" participated generously in the financial part of the program, as it was hoped he would.

A Quick Response

When I was chairman in Philadelphia and southeastern Pennsylvania for a Bucknell University campaign, a Philadelphia alumnus dropped in to see me about that campaign. He was a bond salesman and had some very good customers. He said, "You know I cannot talk bonds to these people all the time and I have to talk to them about other things, so I very often talk to them about Bucknell. As a result, one man has become very much interested in the college. Would you go out with me and chat with him about the campaign?" I gladly agreed.

We arranged a luncheon at a Philadelphia club. Those attending were the bond salesman alumnus, his customer, one of Bucknell's trustees and myself. We talked about the campaign. I explained to them how it was going. The customer friend of the alumnus turned around to me and said, "Do you have a card for me?" I answered, "I don't have any card with your name on it, but in a campaign I always carry a lot of cards and will be very glad to let you make one out." Since I had just met the man, I thought we would be very fortunate to get a subscription anywhere from $100 to $1,000.

He wrote out the card, signed it, and handed it to me. Not to be too inquisitive, I stuck it in my pocket without reading

it, but of course thanked him for it. We adjourned our luncheon. When we got out on the street, I reached into my pocket
and pulled out his card and to my amazement found a subscription for $50,000—one of the quickest subscriptions I have ever
received.

This generous man ultimately became chairman of the board
of trustees at Bucknell and was an active leader with Dr.
Arnaud C. Marts during the latter's presidency of the university. Bucknell named its beautiful new English department
building for this generous trustee, after his decease—the
Charles P. Vaughan Literature Building.

A Big Surprise

As we were counseling Cornell University, in 1948, we found
that the president, Dr. Day, was so much averse to taking part
in any fund-raising effort that he had put it in his written con-
tract with the university that he was not to take part in any
such effort. When we learned this, we knew that we had a
difficult problem on our hands, because the president of an
institution needs to provide top leadership in a fund-raising
program.

Dr. Day was a very able president and very cooperative and
effective in the administrative and academic duties of the university; but he clung to his decision not to take part in raising
money. I finally asked him to see a particular individual without asking for any money, saying, "He is a friend of yours.
He has confidence in you and all I want you to do is to take
this brochure and explain what Cornell is doing and planning."

Double-checking, he said again, "And I am not to ask him
for any money?" I agreed. He did what I asked him to do.
The day after his visit with this gentleman, Dr. Day had a
telephone call from him saying, "Put me down for the cost of
the building on page 17 in the brochure." The cost of the
building was $1,500,000!

From that time on, the president became very much interested and was a great help in fund raising for the university. He had learned in a very pleasant way that fund raising for a great cause is not a begging proposition, but is a dignified, manly and honorable form of public service.

What Will the Money Really Do?

We were asked at one time to counsel a very prominent boys' preparatory school for the purpose of financing a new heating plant. It had tried twice, I think, to raise the funds for this purpose and each time had failed.

They came to us, saying that for some reason or other their constituency did not seem to be interested in a new heating plant. We made a complete survey of the situation and learned what one would naturally expect—that insufficient heat was affecting the health, the efficiency and the comfort of the students. We then put on a program, not primarily to raise funds for a heating plant, but to raise funds for the health, the efficiency and the comfort of the student body, which would be benefited by a new heating plant. The constituency responded generously and the desired heating plant was soon in operation.

Joy from Giving

In the early 1930s I was counseling Southern College in Lakeland, Florida, during a time of a great boom in Florida real estate.

I visited a real estate broker who was very active in buying and selling real estate in that boom and talked to him about a subscription to the college. At that time he occupied the whole floor of a large office building in Lakeland.

He told me that he was just too busy to think about giving anything to the college at that time, indicating he had large-scale ideas about such a gift, but that he did not have time now to work it out. I suggested he defer the working out of the large idea, but at the present time make what he might think was a small gift to the institution. He did. He wrote a check for a four figure amount, saying that he would do the big thing later on.

He never got a chance to do the big thing. The next time I saw him was a year or two after the boom had collapsed, and it had affected him very adversely. Instead of occupying the whole floor of this large office building, he was now occupying one small room in it and had lost practically all of his holdings.

He told me that he did not regret the making of this smaller gift to Southern College, because if he hadn't done it, as he put it, that money would have gone down the drain, too. In fact, he said, "It gave me great satisfaction to remember that I had done some good with some of my property while I still had it."

An Interview Crisis

Every once in a while visiting a person for a gift to an institution produces a difficult problem.

We were counseling the Presbyterian Board of Education and its constituent colleges over the country and among those colleges was the Johnson C. Smith University, a Negro university in North Carolina. Its president was Dr. Hardy Liston. He had been trying for some time to interest the well-known and generous James B. Duke of North Carolina in his college, but had been unsuccessful. Finally, one day he received a telephone call from Duke, who asked him to come up to see him as soon as he could. Dr. Liston was on his way at once and finally was ushered in to see Duke.

They talked generally about the college and its needs. Then Duke revealed that he was thinking of making a distribution of some of his assets before he died, and that he had the Johnson C. Smith University in mind for a part of that distribution. At that moment, he reached in the drawer of his desk and pulled out a box of cigars, offering one to Dr. Liston. It was probably as great a crisis in his life as he ever had, for—as Dr. Liston put it—"There I was trying to get some financial help from one of the wealthiest men in the world who had made his money in tobacco and things related to tobacco, and he was offering me one of the things out of which he made his money. I don't smoke and, of course, for a second or two I hesitated about what to do. Finally I said to him. 'Mr. Duke, I am sorry but I never learned to smoke and I don't think I would know what to do with this cigar. I hope that will have no effect on my conversation with you.'" Duke retorted, "You say you never learned to smoke? Well, don't learn. It is a bad habit." He put his cigars away and the conversation went on in a very fruitful way. Johnson C. Smith University did receive some of Duke's vast generosity.

Big Men Are Available for Service

In the course of my career I counseled the Northern Baptist Convention in a program for the benefit of its schools and colleges. In developing the organization to promote this program, I went to see J. L. Kraft, who was at that time one of the leading officers of his large national corporation. He had built up the Kraft Cheese Company and ultimately became an important part of the national corporation which took his company into a merger.

When I asked him to take the top leadership of this Baptist college program, he said, "No, I cannot do that. I know what you want me for. You want me for my money and I have none available. My wife and I have made up a gift budget for the next ten years showing to whom we are going to give over that period. I don't think it contains any room for a large gift to lead off in a campaign."

I said to him, "No, Mr. Kraft, we don't want you for that. Of course, you will give to this campaign as a member of the Baptist Church, but you will not have to give any greater amount to this campaign as a leader than you would be giving as a member of your church. I will promise you that."

"Then what do you want me to do as chairman?"

"We want people to see you as head of this program. They will then know it is a sound program. When problems come up we will want your experienced judgment. In helping us solve them, you will help us in the leadership of the whole program."

We discussed the matter for a little while and finally he looked at me and said, "You know, I have a notion to believe you. I think I will accept this." And so he did.

About a month later he was in his New York office and called me on the telephone, saying he would like to come down to see me. Naturally, I offered to go up to see him, but he said, "No, I want to come down to see you." When he arrived, I took him into the office of the secretary of the Board of Education, Dr. Luther Wesley Smith, and we had a nice visit about the program. It ended up with his pulling out of his pocket a subscription for $10,000 to start the program off.

When he handed me the subscription, he said, "The thing I like about this program is that it is so clear and simple." He had become convinced that the cause was good and that he could be of real service in it. When a man gets that idea he is glad to give generously to it.

Make Clear a Need

Somebody has said that nobody likes to give away money, but that almost everybody likes to satisfy a human need. It is important, therefore, to lead a person to see what that need is.

I was counseling Whitworth College, in Spokane, Washington. The biggest financial leader in that part of the country was a public utility man whom they called the Owen D. Young of the Northwest, after the late General Electric Company president.

For some reason or other he did not warm up to the Whitworth project and would take no part in it. One day I told him that I would like him to go out to the college and see what they were doing, because I did not think he understood completely what a service to the city it was rendering. He agreed to do this.

We visited the laboratory of the science professor, because that would be most interesting to him. He watched the professor make some experiments and answer some questions, then turned to me and said, "You know I envy this man. He has his work here to do; it is very pleasant and interesting; he comes here at a regular time in the morning; he teaches these students in a quiet way; at the end of the morning, he goes home and engages in reading or studying any other interest he may have; he lives a very orderly and satisfying life; I envy him." I replied, "Now let me tell you something about this fellow. He is married; he has three children, two of whom are in college, and the third is on his way there; he has to pay college charges for his two children; he belongs to the Church and contributes to that; he contributes to the Community Chest; and he is called upon for a number of small incidental financial demands which every citizen has to meet. And to do all of this, how much of a salary do you think he gets?" My friend looked at me and said, "I don't have any idea. How much?" I said, "He gets $2,700 a year. Now do you envy him?"

He looked at me and said, "It is amazing. Is that all he gets?" I answered, "Yes, that is all he gets and that is what this program is for—to increase his compensation to what it ought to be." Thereafter, he took an interested part in the campaign.

Now Back to Mr. Marts's Experiences

$15 Million for Presbyterian Pensions

In 1925 a contributory pension system was recommended to the General Assembly of the Presbyterian Church, U.S.A. (northern). This pension plan had been worked out during previous years on an actuarial basis in order to provide a stated pension under agreed-upon terms to ministers and missionaries of the Presbyterian Church and to their widows, to take the place of the former unpredictable grants of benevolence.

The General Assembly approved the plan and appointed a

committee of twelve highly respected businessmen as the laymen's committee to raise the $15 million fund needed to
launch the pension plan. The Honorable Will H. Hays was
appointed chairman of this committee and the Honorable
Andrew W. Mellon was appointed treasurer. Other members
included the Honorable Robert Lansing, Richard B. Mellon,
Fred E. Weyerhauser, James N. Jarvie and William M. Kingsley. The General Assembly was assured that the $15 million
could be raised from a relatively few people without any wide
appeal being made to churches or to individual members, because it was feared that a wide appeal would disturb and upset
the budgets of the local churches and of the other boards of the
General Assembly.

The laymen's committee asked me to counsel them in this
fund-raising program, so an office was set up convenient to the
office of Will H. Hays in New York City, who was at the time
"Czar" of the Hollywood movie industry. I was given a list
of approximately 200 Presbyterian men and women, each of
whom was said to be able to contribute in six figures to the
needed $15 million basic fund, and I was assured that, for the
most part, they were quite ready to make their contributions to
the needed $15 million as soon as the signal would be given.

It soon became apparent that these persons did not even
know that the General Assembly had authorized a pension plan
for old ministers and missionaries, and I also discovered that
not one of them had any sense of responsibility for providing
any portion of the $15 million needed to launch the pension
system on a sound actuarial basis. We conferred with leaders
of the Presbyterian boards of the General Assembly and were
told that the delegates to the General Assembly would never
have given their consent to an appeal for $15 million if
they had not been assured that it would be contributed by
relatively few people in very large amounts. I found absolutely
no one among the very wealthy Presbyterians, not even among
the responsible laymen's committee men, who was ready to

make a contribution of a size that a total of $15 million would require.

Literature was prepared and distributed among the leaders of the Church and there was a general feeling of satisfaction that a plan had been devised to deal justly with the old servants of the Church upon their retirement. But the optimistic view expressed by some of the leaders to the 1925 General Assembly to the effect "that a handful of wealthy Presbyterian men and women could put up the $15 million between dawn and dusk" proved to be made of the same gossamer stuff as was the famous statement in 1917 by Secretary of State William Jennings Bryan that "a million men would spring to arms in support of the colors in a single day if the nation were in peril."

Having learned the hard way that a handful of wealthy Presbyterian men and women were not going to give this $15 million "at the touch of a push button" it became my duty to report this to Hays and the laymen's committee and to recommend a course of action that, in my judgment, would produce the $15 million launching fund.

When I reported to Hays that we were in a dead-end street under the General Assembly's resolution of 1925, he asked, "What do you propose that we do about it?" I replied that it would be necessary to go before the General Assembly in 1926 and ask for permission to carry the story of the pension fund into every church, and to ask the minister and officers of each church to request the members of their church, individually, and the church, itself, to make contributions to the pension launching fund. Further, I stated that this pension fund could be launched only by the spiritual power and the mass generosity of the members of Presbyterian churches, under the urging of their ministers and elders. It was my opinion that there should be a deep conviction in the rank and file of the denomination that it was the duty of churches and individual members to provide their retiring ministers with a dignified non-charity pension for their old age. In addition, I prophesied that when this ground swell would make itself felt throughout the General Assembly, then, and not until then, would the generous men and women, wealthy and otherwise, of the churches assume their full responsibility in the matter.

Hays looked at me and said, "Who is to make this explanation and request of the 1926 General Assembly?" My answer was, "I am hoping that you will." His eyes blazed, as he said, "You are suggesting that I go before the General Assembly in 1926 and explain that the recommendation of a year ago was wrong and that now we wish to revise it?" I replied, "Yes, for the sake of the old ministers and missionaries and their widows." He thought a moment, then responded, "All right, you write the speech and I will make it."

By the time the General Assembly convened in Baltimore in 1926, word had leaked out that the chairman of the laymen's committee was to ask permission to extend the $15 million appeal to all the people and to all the churches, causing much anxiety prior to that particular session. Some friends of the pension system were so nervous about the opposition that could result that they stayed away from the session. One such leader deliberately walked out of the hall, put on his hat and hurried down the street away from the auditorium when Hays was introduced from the podium.

Hays never blanched. He stood bravely before the General Assembly, delivered his speech, explained the dilemma and asked permission for the laymen's committee to carry the $15 million appeal into every church and to every member. As he finished, there was an outburst of applause. Not a word was spoken in opposition. A motion was made to grant the permission requested, and it was seconded promptly. Discussion was called for, but there was no discussion. The General Assembly voted unanimously to change the nature of the appeal in accordance with Hays' request.

The appeal went forward promptly, presbytery by presbytery, beginning in Philadelphia, then in New York, then westward. When the churches and the ministers and the people stirred themselves in their local communities, large individual contributions, as well as a mass of smaller gifts, were offered. Large individual contributions came from the members of the original laymen's committee and from hundreds of other wealthy Presbyterian men and women. Individual gifts from the members of the laymen's committee were in amounts ranging from $25,000 to $50,000 to $250,000 up to one family contribution of $750,000. It was interesting to observe that *not one of these generous gifts to the pension fund was made until the appeal reached the presbytery in which the donor held his church membership.*

When the appeal was being organized in the Middle West, I asked a member of the staff by the name of Nesbit to call upon a wealthy Presbyterian in his area who was a nominal member of a Presbyterian church, but otherwise was regarded in the community as a "diamond in the rough." When Nesbit visited him and told him of his purpose, "Mr. Diamond in the Rough" said, "Your name is Nesbit. That was the name of the pastor of my beloved sainted mother. She had deep respect for him, and I will always remember him for his influence upon our family and concern for our welfare. Take this check for $100,000 back to headquarters and tell Will Hays and Andrew Mellon that if they had sent someone else without the name of Nesbit, I probably would have given the matter only a passing thought."

It ended successfully on the Pacific Coast with a burst of enthusiasm at the General Assembly in the auditorium in San Francisco in 1927. After 200 years of the Presbyterian Church's concern for the old age of its ministers and missionaries an actuarily sound contributory system of retiring pension was promptly put into operation.

From Counselor to College President

During the early years of my career I counseled colleges, hospitals, churches and other organizations supported by the generosity of Americans. In 1935 I had a college presidency unexpectedly thrust upon me, and I was quickly required to take my own fund-raising medicine which I had been prescribing to other presidents and administrators. The circumstances of this sudden detour in the course of my life made it necessary for me to take some very large doses of my own prescriptions.

It started during the 1920s when I had counseled Bucknell University at Lewisburg, Pennsylvania, in two development programs which threw me into association with the trustees of that institution. A few years later, about 1933, I was invited to serve on the board of Bucknell. I accepted the appointment under Dr. Homer P. Rainey, then the president of Bucknell, who later went back to his own alma mater, the University of Texas, as its president.

In 1935 a special emergency meeting of the board of trustees was called on very short notice for the purpose of acting upon the resignation of Dr. Rainey who had been asked to head the American Youth Commission which was to be a study of the needs of American youth financed by a grant from the Rockefeller Foundation. The resignation was accepted, and the board then proceeded to elect me president of Bucknell—in my absence!

The committee called on me the next day to notify me of this action, and I promptly declined as I had no desire to leave my business and my partners, or to move my home. Other negotiations followed, and I was finally persuaded by the board to become acting president for a period of a year during which time I would spend two days a week at the college and the balance of the time at my office in New York.

This arrangement went on for two years; then I was presented with a petition signed by every student in the college and every member of the faculty asking me to drop the adjective "acting" from my title and to become president of Bucknell. I finally agreed to do this, but with the understanding that I would continue the part-time arrangement previously in force. This I did until July 1, 1945, although during the war years of 1941-1945 I also entered the cabinet of Governor Arthur H. James and Governor Edward Martin at Harrisburg as executive director of the State Council of Defense. Then in January, 1943, I was commissioned as Captain in the U. S. Coast Guard Reserve in charge of the Division of Temporary Reserves in the U. S. Coast Guard with headquarters at Washington.

My first job on the presidential side of the desk at Bucknell was to raise $500,000 to rebuild "Old Main" which had burned down a couple of years previously. That was scarcely accomplished when I was informed by the Engineering Council of Professional Development that I would have to reorganize the engineering courses and build a new chemical engineering laboratory in order to retain the accreditment of the engineering courses. Then came the necessity for a new gymnasium, a new library and the transformation of the Bucknell Junior College at Wilkes-Barre into a fully accredited four-year college, which is now called Wilkes College.

In the presidential office at Bucknell University I soon discovered, or rather had reemphasized, some of the basic principles of generous giving to colleges. These experiences profoundly affected my subsequent counsel to hundreds of other college presidents.

Bucknell's "Old Main" had been destroyed by fire two or three years previously, and the ruins of this historical building at the center of the campus were depressing to the spirits of all, including the students, parents, alumni, faculty and visitors. At my very first trustee meeting I recommended that they proceed immediately to raise the funds necessary to rebuild "Old Main." The recommendation was voted immediately and unanimously, and at the end of my first week as president, I found I had the fund-raising job that faces so many other college presidents.

That evening after the meeting was over and the board members had dispersed, I sat alone in the president's home thinking about who was going to give the needed funds. Naturally, I mentally canvassed the trustees and discovered that I could count on only two of the twenty-five whose generosity could or would reach five figures. Suddenly, I realized why the vote of approval had been so prompt and unanimous. I said to myself, "You walked into a good trap. Your fellow trustees eagerly voted *you* the privilege of raising a half million dollars from *someone else*. Fine fellows as they are, twenty-three of the twenty-five are unable financially to be of any substantial help. Now you have the job to do, but you will have to find most of your support elsewhere." This lesson sank in deeply. I resolved to do the job somehow of rebuilding "Old Main." I further resolved that when the next emergency at Bucknell should arise requiring substantial generosity there would be at least twelve or fifteen members of the board of trustees who could do something far more than cast a vote authorizing me to go out and find someone else to provide the funds for doing it.

I let it be known among alumni and parents that I would like to learn of men worthy in their own lives and spirits to be trustees of Bucknell University and who were generous to causes providing education for ambitious boys and girls.

The nominations that began to come to me of men of this kind were amazing in quality and number, and I was soon able to build up a blacklog of potential trustees that enabled me to add great strength to Bucknell University through its board, as vacancies occurred in the normal course of events.

The next financial emergency burst on me late at night about two years later, when Dr. Joseph W. Barker—then dean of engineering of the University of Columbia and chairman of a visiting committee appointed by the Engineering Council for Professional Development—phoned me from a hotel a few miles distant and asked me to visit him at once on an important matter, which he was under instructions not to discuss with me on the Bucknell campus lest the hospitality offered him might compromise his mission.

I visited him in the middle of the night, and he broke the

news to me that the E. C. P. D., which was in the process of evaluating for accreditment the engineering colleges of the United States, had completed their evaluation of the engineering departments of Bucknell and that he had bad news for me. He would give one-year provisional accreditment to the three departments—mechanical, civil and electrical—but during this one-year period it would be necessary for me to achieve certain internal reorganizations and to provide expanded and improved laboratory space and equipment. As to the Department of Chemical Engineering, the American Chemical Society would withhold accreditment until I could provide an entirely new building for the department with modern laboratories and classrooms. The total cost would be over $1 million. Dr. Barker was a friendly man who understood the seriousness of the report he had made to me and expressed several times his sympathy with me in my predicament. I thanked him sincerely for the spirit of his report, but waived his sympathy and assured him that the $1 million would be no problem, for I had a dozen trustees on my reorganized board whose generosity would take care of that with little public activity or notice.

What happened? Bucknell's four engineering departments were soon fully accredited without any interruption of their prestige, and a splendid new chemical engineering building sprang up miraculously on the campus.

If this volume were a history of Bucknell University I should devote a chapter to certain trustees, whose generosity brought Bucknell so promptly and completely from the ashes of its "Old Main" building to its present magnificent campus. There would be a chapter for each of the following: Daniel C. Roberts, retired associate of Frank W. Woolworth of the great merchandising chain which bears his name; Senator Andrew J. Sordoni of Wilkes-Barre; Michael L. Benedum, oil magnate of Pittsburgh; Robert L. Rooke, investment broker of New York City. I daresay the generosity of these men is being well told in a history of Bucknell University now in the process of publication, written by Dr. J. F. Oliphant, retired professor of history at Bucknell.

One generous act—which resulted from my efforts to bring on our board persons with the right cultural and spiritual qualities plus the capability for great generosity—was an act by the late Mrs. Ellen Clarke Bertrand of New York.

A few months after I had made known my desire to find future trustees who would direct their own generosity to Bucknell, a very loyal alumnus by the name of Joseph Dent, who worked in the Fifth Avenue Branch of the Guaranty Trust Company just across Fifth Avenue from my own office, phoned and asked if he could come over to see me. Upon arrival he asked if I was still receiving nominations for future generous trustees for Bucknell University. After I assured him that I was, he said, "I have a candidate for your consideration." He told me of Mr. and Mrs. Bertrand, indicating he thought Mr. Bertrand was a man with qualities which would make him very valuable as a trustee of Bucknell. Mr. Bertrand was a graduate of Yale, but Yale had never called on him for any special service, and no other college had ever invited him to serve on its board. Dent set up a luncheon at which I was introduced to Bertrand. He was a gentleman with a real interest in education and with the energy and dedication to serve an educational institution that might appeal to him. I asked him, "Would you consider becoming a trustee of Bucknell University, if invited to?" He answered, "I would like to think that over and discuss it with Mrs. Bertrand; perhaps we can meet again in two or three months to canvass the matter further." A few months later Dent reported that Bertrand had been stricken with pneumonia and had died. It seemed to be the end of that particular effort to win a good trustee for Bucknell, but I was wrong—it proved to be just the beginning.

Meanwhile, I had announced that Bucknell greatly needed a new enlarged library, a project already started by Daniel C. Roberts, who had given me $250,000 worth of Woolworth stock as a start for the $750,000 library. When I asked him if he wished it named for him, he said, "Certainly not! They have named one building there for me and one building is enough." I pursued the matter, asking, "Do you have someone else you would like to have it named for?" The answer: "Yes, for you." With a laugh I turned the idea aside and assured him that I would be the last man for whom I would name a building at Bucknell. He then said, "All right I will leave it to you. Name it for anyone you want to, but here is the stock that will give you a good start." With this background, Dent mentioned it to Mrs. Bertrand. Subsequently, he came to me and asked if Bucknell would name the library for Mrs. Bertrand's husband and herself—if she would provide the balance of the funds needed. She said she had remembered, over the years, with great pleasure my conversation with her husband about becoming a trustee at Bucknell—both had appreciated it deeply. Personally, I approved; but since I was no longer president of Bucknell (I had terminated my ten years presidency in 1945), I referred Dent to my successor, the late President Herbert Spencer, who heartily agreed to give the library the desired name.

Mrs. Bertrand proceeded to provide the funds for the cost of the library which at that time greatly exceeded the original estimate. She, herself, was elected to the board of trustees, and she served faithfully and well for the rest of her life. But, that is not the end of the Bertrand generosity! Three or four years ago, I walked into the Fifth Avenue Branch of the Guaranty Trust Company; the manager stepped up to me, with hand outstretched and a big smile, and said, "Have you heard the good news for Bucknell? We are clearing the will of Mrs. Bertrand and she has left her residuary estate to Bucknell." The total proved to be almost $5 million. Thus, an invitation to a gentleman of high quality and generous habits to become a member of a board of trustees of a college (a college which he had *never seen*) resulted in abundant generosity to that college.

Is it any wonder that after my experiences at the presidential desk at Bucknell University, I counseled scores of other college presidents in subsequent years to look for candidates as trustees who could do great things for their colleges?

Another lesson I learned at Bucknell was this: It is extremely easy for a college president to find and enlist such trustees, if he will begin to look for the kind of men who may not be invited by other colleges to serve on their boards and who have a deep unexpressed desire to be of service to a college in that capacity. Many colleges follow the beaten paths to men already serving on other college boards rather than look for men who will give their major overflow to the one particular college. There are many such men who are not being asked to serve on any educational and philanthropic boards. At the same time other men serve on too many such boards. I, for instance, am a striking example of the foolishness of colleges that seek trustees, having served at the same time on as many as five different college boards of trustees, plus three other boards of a research, philanthropic and religious institution. It was foolish for me to undertake to do that and equally foolish of the institutions which divided my time and energy in such an impossible manner, but that is the way too many philanthropic institutions build up their boards. Meanwhile, there are hundreds, perhaps thousands, of capable and devoted men and women throughout the nation, who have never been asked by any college to serve on its board and who would be honored and pleased, just as Bertrand was, to be approached for that purpose.

SIR WINSTON CHURCHILL AT THE MID-CENTURY CONVOCATION OF MASSACHUSETTS INSTITUTE OF TECHNOLOGY

One of the most exciting experiences in my career in American generosity was the occasion when Sir Winston Churchill addressed the M. I. T. Mid-Century Convocation in Boston, Massachusetts.

That great educational institution at Cambridge, Massachusetts, had planned a vast development program which called for gifts and grants totaling $20 million and more. The late Dr. Karl T. Compton was chairman of the M. I. T. corporation, and Dr. James R. Killian was the president. Alfred P. Sloan was honorary chairman of the development committee, and Marshall Dalton was the general chairman. It was a "power team" of leaders, as indeed it had to be for a $20 million program for a single institution fifteen years ago. A most unique and challenging undertaking at that time, it seems relatively small in 1965.

M. I. T. asked me to counsel in this program. As the organization was shaping up, it became apparent that large expectations required comparably large plans, so the officers of the institute decided to hold a convocation of great merit and usefulness which would explore the scientific and intellectual and spiritual progress which Western man had made in the first half of the fabulous twentieth century, and which would consider how he might accelerate his progress in the second half of the century.

M. I. T. named it the Mid-Century Convocation and invited panels of distinguished scholars, scientists, historians, teachers and businessmen to discuss the state of civilization at the half-century milepost; and for the general public session in the evening, the officers invited Sir Winston Churchill to be the speaker.

The original plan was to hold the general evening session in M. I. T.'s own auditorium, but the first day's response to the invitations proved that the auditorium would not accommodate the audience; so, it was decided to move the evening session to M. I. T.'s new gymnasium. Again, before a week was over, the response was so voluminous that the gymnasium was declared too small for the audience. Consequently, it became necessary to move the evening session to the Boston Garden which had the largest seating capacity in greater Boston— 18,000. All the tickets were promptly applied for and issued, yet messages continued to pour in from all over the world—by mail, telegram, radiogram, telephone—all requesting tickets for thousands more seats than were available.

To paraphrase one of Sir Winston's own phrases: Never have

so many been so anxious to travel so far to see and hear and honor one man.

Never have I experienced a spell, almost magical in nature, like that which enveloped Churchill on the platform and his 18,000 listeners in the Boston Garden. We seemed to be of one mind, one mood, one personality.

When the time came to adjourn, Churchill started to leave the podium, he turned toward the steps and waved his well-known V. The audience sprang to its feet, waved arms and let out roars of pent-up emotion. He returned to the podium, faced the vast audience in all directions, waved and turned again toward the steps. Again the throng cried out their devotion. Again he returned to the podium. This was repeated for several minutes, until finally with tears on the cheeks of all, including the guest, Churchill left with a backward smile and wave.

It was a deeply emotional experience which few who were present will ever forget.

The effects of Churchill's visit and appearance at M. I. T.'s Mid-Century Convocation, were both immediate and lasting. The immediate effect was to fill all friends of M. I. T. with new pride in, and enthusiasm for, the institute. As to the more lasting effects, I have heard it said quite frequently that Churchill's visit and the subsequent development program marked the emergence of public recognition of the institute as one of the dozen greatest educational institutions of our age.

XV

M. DE TOCQUEVILLE'S
QUESTION ANSWERED

At the outset of this book, mention was made of the comments which M. de Tocqueville of France made when he observed with surprise, as well as admiration, the American predilection for solving community problems by private initiative and with private funds.

De Tocqueville raised a good question: Is this generosity just a matter of impulse and chance; or is there some inherent relationship between democratic equality and the voluntary association of citizens for the public welfare?

De Tocqueville's question deserves an answer, since he was an outstanding student and philosopher of his day, astute in the nature and processes of democracy.

Comte Alexis Charles Henri Maurice Clérel de Tocqueville, a Frenchman of liberal and democratic convictions, was born in 1805 and began a promising career in public life which lead him through turbulent revolutionary years to the vice-presidency of the French National Assembly and to the Ministry of Foreign Affairs.

While still quite a young man (1831) he was given a mission to visit America and study the prisons in the republic. Pennsylvania had developed a system of cellular penitentiaries which interested the French whose practice had been to punish the commission of a major crime by banishing the guilty criminal. De Tocqueville visited the Eastern Penitentiary at Philadelphia, Sing Sing and Auburn prisons in New York State, and prisons in New England, Michigan and other states. Upon his return to France he made his prison report to his government, of course, but in addition he published the first and greatest of his major works, *Democracy in America* (1835). It was the first published expert analysis of democratic government in America by a competent visitor. During the balance of his life he continued to write, and his complete works, including correspondence, filled nine volumes when they were published after his death in 1859.

De Tocqueville was the first and ablest writer of the middle nineteenth century to present a clear, accurate and appreciative account of the liberal democratic ideals which were dominant in America and which were developing in western Europe and Great Britain in that period.

Certain of de Tocqueville's observations about freedom in America are relevant to this study. He concluded: When a social need became evident and urgent a citizen and his neighbors would probably form a committee (de Tocqueville called it *an association*). They would "not consult a bureaucrat" but would proceed to work at the problem on their own initiative and to put up the needed money out of their own pockets to solve the problem. If a school or a hospital was needed, they would decide where to build it and would find the money needed. When they became disgusted with slavery, they would organize anti-slavery societies. When the women thought they were not being fairly treated, some of them would form an association for women's rights. He remarked that they were "a strange people" in that regard, but a happy nation. He concluded that the health of a democratic nation could be measured by the quality of functions performed by its private citizens.

Thus, de Tocqueville asked: Is all this activity of private

citizens for the public good just a matter of "impulse and chance?" Is there some inherent relationship between democratic equality and this wide-spread initiative which the private citizens of all sections pursue for the public good?

The devotion of de Tocqueville to democracy leads to the conclusion that his question was not raised to be answered, but was in reality a restatement of his positive convictions. It is a Socratic question, patterned after the pedagogy of the ancient teacher of Greece. Socrates threw such questions at his students to challenge them to state in their own phrases the truths which he was trying to teach them.

We believe that all the pages of analytical history of private generosity which lie between his question in Chapter I and this Chapter XV are an answer, in truth, to the first half of the question. American private generosity for the public good is *not* a matter of impulse or chance; it is just the opposite! It is the inevitable flowering of the very best moral, spiritual and cultural aspirations, insights, experiences and inspirations, over nineteen centuries, of all the various racial strains that have merged in the creation of Western man.

Now, for the second half of M. de Tocqueville's question: Is there some inherent relationship between private generosity for the public good and democratic equality? There is a very close and vital relationship. Where, but in an open society of free, self-governing people could a committee of private citizens decide to build a school, a hospital, a boys' club, a college? In what non-democratic nation could a labor union or a chamber of commerce organize, write its own by-laws, and manage its own program? Where, except in an open society of free people could private citizens form an association to oppose slavery or to advocate free public schools?

We have such freedoms in America, and use them daily to advance social and cultural improvements of an almost endless range. We might well call such freedoms "the freedoms *to*" distinguished from our other basic "freedoms *from*."

The "freedoms *from*" assure us as individuals of the protec tion of our life, liberty and property from internal tyranny and from external attack.

The "freedoms *to*" give us the privilege of using our talents in voluntary association with other private citizens to initiate social and cultural improvements for the public good.

THE BILL OF RIGHTS

The founding fathers expressly provided for our "freedom *to*" in the Bill of Rights, ratified in 1791.

Article IX.

The enumeration in the Constitution of certain rights shall not be construed to deny or disparage others retained *by the people*.

Article X.

The powers not delegated to the United States by the Constitution, nor prohibited by it to the States are reserved to the states respectively *or to the people*.

This is American generosity's Magna Carta for "freedom to." This is legal sanction for the private generosity and initiative for the public good which the early settlers had been practicing diligently ever since they began to arrive in the 1620s.

Here, government gave its full confidence and freedom to its citizens to use their enthusiasm and their private means to create a better nation.

It is of this "freedom to" that Lowell wrote:

> Freedom is re-created year by year
> In hearts wide open on the Godward side.
> True freedom is to share
> All the chains our brothers wear.

American generosity is the flowering of that freedom "to share all the chains our brothers wear." It is the evidence that 40,000,000 Americans desire to have a part in creating a better world.

SUPPLEMENT

Introduction

An analytical history requires the author to rush the reader through quite a wide expanse of time and geography with blinders on, so that the latter will not become too much interested in (or the author too prolix concerning) other exciting events which are happening right beside the path being followed. Having some of that single-mindedness of the bloodhound which sniffs its way toward its quarry without much attention to anything but the spoor and the trail, the author felt obliged to act just that way, in apparent ignorance of events, here and there, which were of greater general importance than some contemporaneous events which were noted and described.

Consequently, this section is added as supplemental readings, using brief excerpts and comments which amplify certain phases of the civilizing of Western man.

1. JEWISH CHARITY BEFORE CHRIST

Charity was not a virtue invented by the Christians; it was, rather, taught to Jesus and his apostles and the early Christian fathers while they were still practicing Jews—before the Christian religion was born.

From the days of early recorded history, the Jews practiced an effective technique of charity—the tithe. The tenth part of the yield of the harvest was to be given to the Lord, in support of religion and for the relief of the poor. Every seventh year, the people were required to let their fields lie fallow and the poor were permitted to garner the spontaneous growth during the sabbatical year. At every harvest a corner of each field was left unharvested, for the poor. There are those today who feel that the tithe technique has not been improved upon and who earnestly urge a renewal of the practice.

The Pentateuch commanded charity for the unfortunate

members of society and insisted that benevolence was a moral law, not a matter of whimsical choice. All through the history of the Jewish race righteousness has found practical and fervid expression in charity. The "Cell of Silence" or "Chamber of Whispers" was a later Jewish technique which came near to being the ideal exercise of charity. This name was given to a quiet room in the synagogue into which the philanthropic stole —unobserved—and left donations for the respectable poor, who stole in—also unobserved—to obtain the help they needed.

These instructions as to charity were passed down faithfully in the Hebrew Torah, guiding the Jews who have been recognized and acclaimed over all generations for their charity. Jesus, Peter, Paul, and all the founding fathers of the Christian Church were Jews. According to one source[1] all of the first fifteen bishops of the early Christian Church in Jerusalem were circumcised Jews. All of the founding fathers of the Christian Church had learned well the Mosaic lessons of charity. Thus, early Christian charity was not a new thing in itself. What was new was the energy and activity of the Christians in extending their generous charity, their love for mankind, out into their communities to all needy persons.

For the early Christians were evangelizers, eager to take the "good news" to others. The Hebrews have not been evangelizers or proselyters, but they have treasured their religious faith and practices within their own racial and family circles and have been content not to preach or extend it abroad.

This non-proselyting, non-colonizing racial predilection of the first century Jews left the responsibility for pioneering Western civilization to the Christians of the first century. Under the leadership of Christians such as Peter, Paul, Mark, Barnabas and Timothy—each a circumcised Jew—charity, "love of man for the sake of God," became the basic Judeo-Christian virtue of the burgeoning Western civilization.

---

[1] Gibbon, *op. cit.*

The Eight Degrees of Charity

The late Dr. Charles Homer Haskins[2] referred to books produced in the twelfth century as "Cathedrals of Thought." The authors of some of those books were: Peter Comeston, 1150; Petrus Canton, 1190; Thomas Aquinas, 1142; Peter Lombard, 1160; John of Salisbury, 1159; Abelard, 1142—all Christian philosophers.

To his list, the author would add the name of a famed Jewish philosopher, Rabbi Moses Ben Maimon, born in Cordova, Spain, in 1135 of the learned group of Sephardic Jews.

Maimonides, as he is known in history, produced a new codification of the charitable duties of Hebrews which he called "The Eight Degrees of Charity," a remarkable contribution to the literature of charity, as follows:

> First, high degree, than which there is no higher, is that of one who takes hold of an Israelite who has become impoverished and gives him a gift or a loan or goes into partnership with him or finds work for him, in order to strengthen his hand so that he may be spared the necessity of appealing for help.
>
> Less than this (i. e. next below in rank) is the case of one who gives charity to the poor, without knowing to whom he gives and without the poor knowing from whom he takes.
>
> Less than this is the case of the one who knows to whom he gives without the poor knowing from whom he receives. An example of this is the practice of distinguished wise men who used to go secretly and leave money at the doors of the poor.
>
> Less than this is the case where the poor man knows from whom he takes but the giver does not know the receiver. An example of this is the practice of the wise who used to wrap up money in their cloaks and cast the bundles back of them (without looking), the poor coming afterward to pick them up, thus being spared all shame.

---

[2] *The Renaissance of the 12th Century* (New York and Cleveland: World Publishing Company, 1957).

Less than this is the case of him who gives without being asked.

Less than this is the case of him who gives after he is asked.

Less than this is the case of him who gives less than is proper but in a pleasant manner.

Less than this is the case of him who gives reluctantly.

2. WHY DID EARLY CHRISTIANITY EXPAND CHIEFLY WESTWARD?

Jesus' disciples undertook to obey His command (to preach the "good news" to all peoples) in Jerusalem, right at home. Several thousands were won to Jesus' Gospel, but they aroused the anger of certain temple officials and were forced out of the city.

Where else, then, should they continue their evangelistic efforts? In which direction should they go first in order to fulfill Jesus' command to carry His Gospel to all peoples (especially in the year 31 A. D. when the Roman Empire was in command of all nations around the Mediterranean Sea)?

These disciples were all practicing Hebrews; they worshiped in the synagogues and observed the Hebrew laws; they were permitted to speak publicly in many synagogues; and there was even some expectation that Christianity might become a sect of the Jewish religion.

Surely the disciples must have thought of the possibility of starting their journeys for the extension of Jesus' Kingdom of Heaven eastward through Syria and Arabia, to the Semitic lands from which Abraham's father had originally come to make his permanent home in Palestine. A few of them did, indeed, start eastward. Four of the Apostles, Thaddeus, Bartholomew, Simon and Jude, were believed to have preached the Gospel in Armenia, and to have been martyred there.[3] Their missionary labors laid the earliest foundations for Armenia becoming the first Christian nation on Earth (303

---

[3] Herbert J. Muller, *The Loom of History* (New York, Harper & Brothers, Publishers, 1958).

A. D.) when their king, Tiridates III was converted to the faith by St. Gregory, the Illuminator. Armenia's example was followed by Constantine, first Christian emperor of Rome, a few years later.

St. Thomas *did* turn eastward on his missionary tour and carried Jesus' "good news" back to Parthia, east of the Euphrates and Tigris Rivers, where it is believed that Abraham's ancestors had dwelt. Eusebius called Thomas the "Evangelist of Parthia," and some of his bones are preserved in Edessa, the Parthian city, reported to have been brought from India, where Thomas was said to have been martyred. "Christians of St. Thomas" is the name still given to the ancient Christian churches of southern India. A shrine to Thomas' martyrdom was built near Madras, showing a cross with a Pahlive inscription which dates back to the seventh century. It still stands on Mt. St. Thomas, after being restored by the Portuguese in 1547.

Some of the disciples probably thought that Egypt would be a suitable starting place for their evangelizing efforts, because it was nearby and had been the birthplace of their great prophet Moses; but they did not turn immediately in that southern direction either. Mark did go to Egypt years later, after he had gone the whole western route with Peter and Paul —to the end of their lives at Rome.

But the most successful early Christian missionaries chose the westward routes, probably for two major reasons. First, "all roads lead to Rome"; secondly, because Asia Minor had been infiltrated by Grecian, or Hellenistic, culture which drew the missionaries toward Greece, the southeastern tip of modern Europe.

THE HELLENIZATION OF ASIA MINOR

The 1,000 year history of Asia Minor (the area east of the Mediterranean Sea) may be summarized by saying that for centuries this rich and desirable area had been fought over and ruled successively by several empires—Babylon, Egypt,

Chaldea, Persia, Greece and Rome. Alexander the Great had won it from Persia for Greece about 340 B. C., and the Greeks had thoroughly infiltrated the people of the area, including the Hebrews in Palestine. Long after Rome had taken the area away from Greece, the Greek culture, language and people remained. In other words, Asia Minor had been Hellenized. Greece, in turn, had been influenced by oriental faiths after Alexander had overcome the eastern empires and his soldiers had returned with new ideas. The oriental faiths appealed more strongly to the masses than had the ritualistic worship of all the Greek gods which satisfied the rich and cultured Grecians.

Christianity followed in the wake of this post-Alexandrian invasion of oriental faiths and was welcomed by the Hellenized people of Asia Minor, and by the Greeks themselves, because of its universal appeal to all persons, rich and poor, mighty and lowly, free and slave.

Christianity appropriated some of the terms and worship practices of the Grecian religion, but ultimately displaced and destroyed it.

THE HELLENIZATION OF THE HEBREWS

In addition to the general efforts of Alexander and his successors to infiltrate Greek culture, language and ideas into the life of all the nations which the Macedonians had conquered, special ties were created between Greeks and Jews.

For instance, after Alexander the Great had conquered his world, he wished to leave a great city with his name on it as a permanent memorial to himself, so he founded Alexandria in Egypt at the mouth of the Nile and lavished upon its architecture and adornment all the graces which he could devise, including the great library which became the center of the Mediterranean world's wisdom and culture.

He needed a variety of good citizens also, and, among others, he imported a colony of Jews from Judaea and provided a well-equipped section of his city for them where they could observe their traditional way of life with convenience and without disturbance.

Other evidences of friendship and respect between Greeks and Jews are also to be observed. In 309 B. C., for example, Areus, King of Sparta, had written to the high priest in Jerusalem, Onias, that "it is found in writing that the Spartans and the Jews are brethren, and that they are of the stock of Abraham" (I Maccabees XII. 21).

This intimation of kinship came also from the Jewish side in 144 B. C. when the high priest Jonathan wrote the Spartans that the long-standing friendship between Spartans and Jews was based on ancient kinship.

In short, by the year 31 A. D., when Peter and Paul and the other disciples were about to start their travels to carry Jesus' "good news" to all peoples, they started out northward through *present* friends, the Greco-Jews, rather than eastward or southward toward traditional racial sources.

They were to register their first great successes in cities in Asia Minor which had been well Hellenized, and after that in Grecian cities on the mainland of Europe.

EARLY CHRISTIAN MISSIONARIES

Peter

The Acts of the New Testament fail to give much detail about the course Peter, the energetic leader of Jesus' apostles, took on his missionary journeys after he led the forming of the church at Jerusalem. Accounts indicate that he and John preached in many communities in Samaria and that they persuaded many to become believers in Christ; then, he walked several miles to the seacoast where he had a vision at Joppa, which helped to set the whole future course of "The Path." [4]

---

[4] The term was inspired by a footnote in Arnold J. Toynbee's *Greek Civilization and Character* (New York: New American Library, 1954). "The Path" is one of the names by which the Christian persuasion was familiarly known among its members.

The vision was revealed to Peter, in a strange allegory, that Jesus' Gospel was meant not for Jews alone, but for all men. Obeying this command, Peter went northward along the coast to Caesarea, where he converted Cornelius, the resident Roman centurion and his whole family.

Continuing "The Path" Peter and Barnabas went to Antioch, almost to the extreme northeast corner of the Mediterranean, where, according to Eusebius, Peter established the Christian Church and see (35 A. D.). It was there that Jesus' followers were first called Christians.

Peter then took the western path. He helped to establish churches at Ephesus on the eastern shore of the Aegean Sea. Then, about 42 A. D., he personally took the plunge into Europe. He crossed the Aegean Sea into Greece; stayed awhile with the church at Corinth; then moved on to the shining goal —Rome, the capital of the Western world, arriving, it is presumed, during the reign of Claudius as emperor (41-50 A. D.). A tradition traceable to Jerome (344 A. D.) says that Peter resided in Rome for twenty-five years, though not in an uninterrupted sojourn. In any event, he was back in Jerusalem (in 49 or 50 A. D.) for a council with the other apostles to adjust differences of opinion. Tradition also claims that Peter found a small Christian community at Rome (40 A. D.) consisting of Jewish and pagan converts; it may have been assembled by one of many early converts who carried the Gospel to Rome on a business visit to the capital city.

It is historically accepted that Peter served as the first bishop of the see of Rome, and that he met death there during the persecutions of Nero, perhaps 64 or 67 A. D. It is believed that he was buried at the foot of the Vatican Hill, where under Constantine the Great, a church was erected in his honor and where today stands the great basilica of St. Peter. Eusebius relates that Peter met his death by crucifixion, and, at his own request, with his head down, in humble honor to his Lord, Jesus.

"The Path" had reached Rome, the head and heart of Western civilization, and all along its course had taught men the virtue and the practice of love and generosity toward their fellowmen.

Paul

The great missionary-apostle Paul is the same zealous rabbinical student, Saul, a native of Tarsus, who had joined the mob which stoned Stephen to death in Jerusalem in the year 30 A. D. Then, he went to Damascus to lead the persecution of Jesus' followers in that city, but he was struck blind en route and experienced a vision of Jesus, who called upon Saul to follow Him.

Saul yielded and joined the little Christian group at Damascus, but they—as well as the Christians at Jerusalem—feared him. Consequently, Saul took refuge somewhere in Arabia to think over his new life, later returning to his home at Tarsus, where he stayed quietly for six years, pursuing his trade as a tentmaker and preaching occasionally in his synagogue. Barnabas, however, remembered him and sought him out, persuading him to go to the new church at Antioch, not far away, to teach and preach. Before long, Paul became a powerful and persuasive evangelist for Christ.

In 45-47 A. D. Paul set out on his first and second missionary journeys—westward around the area of the northern shores of the Mediterranean Sea. First he went to Cyprus, to Iconium, to the other Antioch in Pisidia, to Ephesus, to Troy, over the Aegean Sea to Thessalonica, Corinth and Philippi, in Greece and Europe. And, in 57 A. D., he even dared to stand up on Mars Hill in Athens, and proclaim Jesus as the "unknown God" they were seeking. Both Peter and Paul had now brought "The Path" into Europe and the assimilation of its Gospel into the mainstream of Western civilization was assured.

Meanwhile, all the missionaries found it necessary to return to Jerusalem for a very urgent conference on an important issue—for a decision could no longer be postponed. The issue was this: Must a convert to Christianity first become a practicing Hebrew before being baptized as a Christian? In other words, must he accept the ceremony of circumcision and conform to the dietary laws and the other observances of the Mosaic laws?

It was a far-reaching issue. The apostles met in what is known as the Council of Jerusalem about 50 A. D. The result was to free converts outside of Palestine from the yoke of the Hebrew law, with the exception of abstention from "things sacrificed to idols, etc." It was a hard decision for a group of Jewish leaders to make, and it was only completely observed by all after the year 70 A. D. when Titus totally destroyed Jerusalem.

But had it not been made, Jesus' hope that the Kingdom of Heaven on Earth would encompass people of all nations might have perished at that period.

Paul's career ended in Rome, probably in 64 A. D.—he died a martyr.

Barnabas

Barnabas, a nephew of Mary in whose home the first church in Jerusalem held its meetings, was converted to Christianity and turned his fortune over to the apostles for missionary work. It was he who recruited Paul as a missionary, accompanying Paul on at least one of his journeys. He and his cousin, John Mark, went to Cyprus to serve the church there—where, it is believed, he is buried.

Philip

Philip was the first Christian missionary—the one who encountered, on the highway, the Ethiopian eunuch, whom he converted and baptized by the roadside.

Andrew

Andrew was the brother of Simon Peter; fishing partner of James and John; close friend of Philip. After the fall of Jerusalem, he went with John as a missionary to Ephesus, and later preached in Scythia and Achaea where he suffered death by crucifixion on a unique cross, called "decussata"—now called a St. Andrew's Cross.

St. Andrew is the legendary founder of the Greek Orthodox Church; and, according to the legend, the present ecumenical patriarch of the Greek Orthodox Church at Constantinople, Athenogoras I, is the 261st successor of St. Andrew, just as Pope Paul VI, head of the Roman Catholic Church at Rome, is the 261st successor of Andrew's brother, Peter.

John Mark

John Mark, the son of Mary, was one of Peter's converts who went with Paul and his cousin, Barnabas, on Paul's first missionary journey, but later went to Rome with Peter, as the latter's secretary. It is believed he wrote the second Gospel of the New Testament while at Rome.

After Peter's death in Rome, John Mark went to Alexandria, Egypt, to which city a strong Jewish colony had been imported 300 years earlier by Alexander the Great. There John Mark established a Christian church which, in the course of time, developed into a very important see of the Eastern or Greek Orthodox Church. He died there, probably a martyr. Centuries later his body was brought to Venice by some of that city's far-ranging Christian merchants, and the present beautiful Cathedral of St. Mark in Venice treasures John Mark's remains in its resplendent golden altar.

Why did Peter, Paul and the other apostles make these efforts? What was the evangelizing, energizing force in the Christian religion which thrust Peter and Paul and the other apostle missionaries out into the Western world with their zeal to win converts and to change the lives of men and of nations? Why did they endure the hardship, and finally even murder and martyrdom to carry Jesus' Gospel to others?

Of his sufferings Paul wrote, "Of the Jews five times received I forty stripes save one. Thrice was I beaten with rods, once was I stoned, thrice I suffered shipwreck, a night and a day have

I been in the deep, in perils of rivers, in perils of robbers, in perils from my countrymen, in perils from the Gentiles, in perils in the city, in perils in the wilderness, in perils in the sea, in perils among false brethren, in labor and travail, in watchings often, in hunger and thirst, in fastings often, in cold and nakedness." Paul probably answered for all his associates with this triumphant declaration: "I take pleasure in injuries, in persecution, in distresses, for Christ's sake."

ISLAM, THE OTHER EVANGELIZING RELIGION OF THAT AREA CHOSE DIFFERENT DIRECTIONS FOR ITS EXPANSION

The other evangelizing religion, Islam, which began not far from Jerusalem, in Mecca six centuries later, chose the exact directions, eastward and southward, which might logically have been selected for the routes of the early Christian evangelists.

Each of these two religions aspired to evangelize the world; each believed in one God; each took the name of its founder (Christ; Mohammed). They were founded within a camel's ride distance from each other. One expanded northward and westward along the northern shore of the Mediterranean Sea; the other expanded eastward in Arabia thence to the Indian Ocean and southward to Egypt, then westward along the entire southern shore of the Mediterranean Sea.

Both of these expansive evangelistic religions reached vast numbers of persons. Today there are said to be 993,000,000 members of Christian churches and 446,000,000 members of Islam.

3. TWO GREAT CHRISTIAN SCHOLARS OF THE FOURTH CENTURY

Jerome

Known as the great Christian scholar of his age, Jerome was born in 340 A. D. of Christian parents at Strido, Dalmatia. Educated in Rome, he spent his Sundays in the catacombs, discovering graves of the martyrs and deciphering inscriptions. Later he toured the east—Athens, Bithynia, Galatea, Antioch.

In 379 A. D. he was ordained a presbyter, and wrote many tracts on philosophy and theology. By 381 A. D. he was brought to Rome by Pope Damascus to revise the "Old Latin" translation of the Bible. His translations of the Gospels, the rest of the New Testament and the Psalms were published in Rome. He left Rome when Siricius became pope (384 A. D.) and went to Bethlehem where two wealthy Roman women, Paula, a widow, and her daughter wished to dedicate their fortune to Christ through generous good works. They built four monasteries—three for nuns, one for monks. Jerome presided over the monks' monastery. Here he did most of his literary work, including a translation of the Old Testament from the Hebrew text. His translations became the Vulgate Bible authorized by the Church, and used as the Roman Catholic Bible for subsequent centuries. Jerome died in Bethlehem in 420 A. D.

St. Augustine

St. Augustine was received as a convert to Christianity by Ambrose, Bishop of Milan, and in 391 A. D. he was ordained as priest of the mission church in Tagaste, Africa. He was consecrated as bishop of Hippo in 396 A. D. and thereby began a series of letters, 220 in all, which were circulated widely to Christian churches in all lands, as Paul's letters had been. His sermons also were collected and became a commentary on the Bible. In all, he issued 230 tracts and larger essays, as well as more than fifty treatises published as books. He was one of the greatest of early Christian scholars, and his book, *City of God,* had a profound effect upon the Christian Church.

St. Augustine's idea of the society of men, dominated and overruled by the Christian Church, is said to have made such a profound impression on Charlemagne (The Great), king of the Franks, that he permitted the Pope to crown him at Rome in 800 A. D. as the first emperor of the Holy Roman Empire. Charlemagne is reported to have believed that the "City of God" would be the fulfillment of Jesus' Kingdom of Heaven on Earth.

St. Augustine's concept of the unity of Christendom held the nations of Europe together for a thousand years, even in times of war with each other, in bonds of restraint and a common loyalty. St. Augustine used his skill in vigorous refutation of pagan criticisms of Christianity. The Christian Church of the late fourth century and thereafter was invigorated and reinforced by the great brain and spirit and genius of this thinker and writer. The following is a typical charge made against Christ and his followers by pagans and the reply by St. Augustine (about 430 A. D.):

> *Pagan charge:* After the sack of Rome by the barbarians in 410 A. D., the decline of the Roman Empire was due to Christ and his church, who made the Roman gods angry.
>
> *St. Augustine's reply:* Anyone can perceive all the losses and disasters, moral and political, which had befallen Rome under its pagan gods before Christ. The city had fallen into a vicious morass before Christ was born. Did anyone impute these great evils to their pagan gods? Before the coming of Christ and after the sack of Carthage, the manners of the upper classes collapsed in a headlong torrent, so corrupted by luxury was the youth of that age. Where were all the gods when Rome was set on fire? Fast asleep? Only the geese on Capitoline Hill stayed awake and alerted the guards. And the Romans began to hold a Goose Fair; they almost began to worship geese, so low was their esteem for their gods.

4. CHRONOLOGICAL LIST OF THE EMPERORS OF THE PAGAN ROMAN EMPIRE (27 B. C. TO 311 A. D.)

As a further aid to understanding the nature of the pagan Roman Empire in its first three centuries, the following chronological list of the emperors of pagan Rome is presented with a brief résumé of the career of each. Obviously, being emperor in those years was an extremely hazardous occupation.

(27 B. C.-14 A. D.) *Augustus Octavian* was a nephew of Julius Caesar, dictator of the Roman Republic, and he became his

heir when Julius Caesar was murdered in 45 B. C. Augustus spent the next ten years in conflict with the contenders; proscribed death for 300 Senators, including Cicero and 2,500 knights. He conquered Antony and Cleopatra, who committed suicide. In 27 B. C. he reconstituted the Republic and was named president. Later, he was given the imperial title—Augustus. His adopted stepson, Tiberius, was named his successor. When he died of illness and old age in 14 A. D., the Senate decreed him a God.

(14-37 A. D.) *Tiberius* was the son of Tiberius Claudius Nero and Livia, who was ceded by her husband to Augustus—who adopted Tiberius. He won many victories as general; he also murdered his brother's widow, Agrippina, and two of her children. H. G. Wells said of Tiberius, "It would seem that he was addicted to gross and abominable vices." His death was mysterious, possibly by murder.

(37-41 A. D.) *Caligula* (Gaius Caesar) was the son of Agrippina and nephew of Tiberius. Probably insane, he was a monster of cruelty and vice who bestowed a consulship on his horse. The earliest of the tradition that later prevailed among Roman emperors, that of the oriental type of monarch, he insisted on personal deification. He was murdered by a tribune of the guard.

(41-54 A. D.) *Claudius* was a nephew of Tiberius and grandson of Livia, wife of Augustus. Underdeveloped, mentally and physically, he was made emperor by the praetorian (on the murder of Caligula) to whom he gave a large donation. He married his niece, Agrippina, as his fourth wife, who induced him to set aside his own son, Britannicus, and to adopt her son, by a former marriage—Nero. Poisoned by Agrippina, he died at age forty-four.

(54-68 A. D.) *Nero* was the son of Agrippina, niece and wife of Claudius, who adopted him. Agrippina poisoned Claudius and presented Nero to the guards as their emperor—all was confirmed by the Senate.

Nero had his mother and wife murdered. When Rome was destroyed by fire in 64 A. D., the provinces were ransacked to raise funds to rebuild the city. Galba claimed the throne, and Nero took refuge from the guards sent to drag him to be executed. He committed suicide. Nero initiated the persecutions of the Christians which were carried on until the close of the third century.

(68-69 A. D.) *Galba*—Servius Sulpicius—was a son of a noble and wealthy family who served Claudius loyally in Gaul and Spain. It was rumored that Nero planned to murder him, but when Nero committed suicide, Galba marched to Rome and was made emperor by the Senate. Otho conspired to have him murdered.

(69 A. D.) *Otho*—Marcus Salvius—was a dissolute member of Nero's court, who had been sent as governor of Lusitania. He went to Rome with Galba hoping to be his successor, but Galba selected Piso. Otho then murdered Galba and Piso, and then had himself declared emperor. The army in Germany declared for Vitellius and Otho led his army to check Vitellius, only to have his army crushed. Otho committed suicide.

(69 A. D.) *Vitellius*—Aulus—was not ambitious, but was proclaimed emperor by the armies of Germany at Cologne. He was accepted by the Senate, but the armies of the east declared for Vespasian. The troups of Vespasian dragged him out of a hiding place, and he was murdered at the fatal Gemonian stairs.

(69-79 A. D.) *Vespasian*—Titus Flavius—the son of a tax collector, had a successful military career in Germany and Britain. He was put in charge of the army and sent to put down the Jewish revolt in Judaea. His army proclaimed him emperor at Caesarea and he marched on Rome to defeat Vitellius and destroy the capitol by fire.

He reorganized the administration of the provinces, and introduced economy and good management to the public treasury. He left two sons, Titus and Domitian.

(79-81 A. D.) *Titus*—Flavius Sabinus Vespasianus—a son of

Vespasian, carried on the siege of Jerusalem which was captured in 70 A. D. He and Vespasian celebrated a triumph, recorded by the *Arch of Titus*. He finished the coliseum in Rome, and the empire was peaceful in his reign. Berenice, sister and wife of Herod Agrippa, came to live in the palace with him, but public opinion forced him to send her back to Judaea. His brother, Domitian, plotted against him, but Titus was lenient.

(81-96 A. D.) *Domitian*—Titus Flavius Domitianus—was a son of Vespasian who lived in retirement while his brother, Titus, reigned, devoting himself to a life of pleasure and literary pursuits. The death of Titus was pleasing to Domitian—in fact, some thought that he helped to bring it about.

Domitian attempted a reform of morals and religion and erected many temples. During the last few years he behaved like a madman; he murdered generals and associates whom he feared; he sentenced his own cousin and nephew to death and banished his wife because he thought her friendly to Christianity. He was stabbed to death in his bedroom by a freedman.

(96-98 A. D.) *Nerva*—Marcus Cocceius—was the son of a senatorial family. Consul under Vespasian and Domitian, he was banished by the latter on a charge of conspiracy. When Domitian was murdered, Nerva was proclaimed emperor by the people and the soldiers. A quiet, kindly, dignified, honest man, he recalled all those who had been banished by Domitian, and restored their property. He instituted public support of the children of poor parents in the towns of Italy and encouraged the *most genuinely charitable institutions* of the pagan world—"the alimentationes."

(98-117 A. D.) *Trajan* was born in Spain the son of an Italian legionnaire who became governor of Asia. He was adopted by Nerva as son and successor. After his military victory, Dacia was annexed to the empire. He also conquered Parthia; and there were revolts in Africa, Egypt, Libya, Palestine and Britain. He built great monuments in Rome—forums, columns, arches, roads, aqueducts. Trajan led Rome another step to complete despotism before he died in bed. He was deified as god.

(117-138 A. D.) *Hadrian*—Publius Aelius Hadrianus—was a kinsman of Trajan. Empress Plotinus arranged a marriage for him with Trajan's grandniece, Vibia Sabina, and upon Trajan's death she claimed that Hadrian had been adopted. The Senate and army proclaimed him emperor. Hadrian abandoned Trajan's far eastern conquests, but carried out Trajan's scheme for "alimentationes" for poor children on a larger scale.

He traveled to all parts of the empire—Gaul, Germany on the Rhine, Britain, Spain, Mauretania, Greece, Parthia, Asia Minor, Syria, Jerusalem, Arabia and Egypt. He adopted Antoninus Pius as his successor, and was one of the most capable of emperors.

(138-161 A. D.) *Antoninus Pius* was adopted by Hadrian on condition that he adopt as his successor, his wife's (Faustina's) nephew, Marcus Aurelius Verus (Marcus Aurelius), and Lucius Verus. He became emperor and begged the Senate to give *divine* honors to Hadrian. His reign was wise and honest.

(161-180 A. D.) *Marcus Aurelius* with Lucius Verus (161-9 A. D.) and with Commodus (177-180 A. D.). Marcus Aurelius married Antoninus' daughter, Faustina. He was engaged by military attacks on all sides. His soldiers, returning from war in Syria, brought a pestilence (165 A. D.) which devastated Europe and Asia. Verus died in 169 A. D. and Marcus ruled alone until his young son, Commodus, joined him in 177 A. D.

He was a Stoic philosopher, author of meditations and gave large sums to endow chairs of philosophy and rhetoric, chiefly in Athens. Under his rule, Christians were persecuted in 177 A. D. He died while with the army in Pannonia, possibly poisoned by Commodus.

"Consistently hostile to Christians; and persecutions, unknown or forbidden under earlier reigns, were systematically pursued under his direction. Reason—the state religions were an essential part of the imperial system and the Christians, particularly in their opposition to emperor worship, were a danger to the established order." (From the *Encyclopædia Britannica*)

(180-192 A. D.) *Commodus*—Lucius Aelius Aurelius—was a son of Marcus Aurelius and Faustina. At the age of fifteen he was associated with his father in the government. In 183 A. D. his sister, Lucille, engaged an assassin to murder him. He became tyrannical and put many distinguished citizens to death. He exhausted the treasury by lavish expenditures on gladiatorial and wild beast combats and confiscated the property of the wealthy. The people rose up in revolt because of the dearth of corn. Several attempts were made on his life. Finally, his chamberlain, Electus; the prefect of the praetorian guards, Laetus; and his mistress, Marcia, found their names on the list of those doomed to death—and murdered him.

(193 A. D.) *Pertinax*—Publius Helvius—was a son of a charcoal burner; became a grammar school teacher; then rose through public offices, civil and military, to consul. He was chosen to succeed Commodus as emperor against his own will because of his advanced age. He was assassinated in a mutiny of the soldiers in March, 193 A. D.

(193 A. D.) *Didius Julianus* was a grandson of a famous jurist under Hadrian and son of a distinguished general. "On the death of Pertinax, the praetorian guards offered the throne of emperor to the highest bidder. Didius and Sulpicianus bid against each other, and the throne was knocked down to Didius for an amount equal to 200 pounds sterling. The Senate and nobles professed their loyalty, but the people resented the insult to the state. Armies revolted and declared Septimius Severus, Commander of the Pannonian legions, emperor. Didius was deserted by the praetorians, and executed by the Senate." (From the *Encyclopædia Britannica*)

(193-211 A. D.) *Severus*—Lucius Septimius—was born of Roman parents in Africa. The legions proclaimed Severus emperor promptly after Julianus was murdered. He defeated the forces of his chief rival, Albinus, in 197 A. D. and declared himself the son of Marcus Aurelius and the brother of Commodus (false). He poured forth his wrath upon the civilian population; arrested sixty Senators, and killed half of them. He married Marcia, and later married Julia Donna. His sons, Caracalla and Geta, hated each other. Julia and Caracalla plotted against him. He died while with the army in England (211 A. D.). He issued an edict against conversion to Christianity.

(211-217 A. D.) *Antoninus Caracalla* with Geta (211-212 A. D.). He was born at Lyons. He and Geta returned to Rome as co-emperors after their father died at York, England. In order to secure sole power, he murdered his brother in 212 A. D. and put to death 20,000 of Geta's supporters. His extravagances and the demands of his soldiers were a perpetual drain; he waged war on the Danube, in Asia, Mesopotamia and Egypt; he ordered a general massacre in Alexandria in revenge for an imagined disrespect; he was murdered at Carrahae by the prefect of the praetorian guards, Opellius Macrinus, who succeeded him as emperor. The baths of Caracalla still adorn Rome.

(217 A. D.) *Macrinus* was made emperor by the praetorians after he had arranged for Martialis, a disappointed soldier, to stab Caracalla to death near the Temple of the Moon in Syria. His attempts to reform the army made him unpopular; and Julia Maesa, sister-in-law of Septimius Severus, announced that her grandson, Elagabalus, was the son of Caracalla. He was declared emperor and assumed the name Antoninus. Macrinus was defeated and killed and Antoninus and his court set out for Rome.

(218-222 A. D.) *Elagabalus (Antoninus)* was licentious beyond description, and lost the respect and support of all. He was persuaded by Maesa, grandmother of his cousin Alexander Severus, to adopt him. The praetorians mutinied and murdered Elagabalus and his mother, Soemias.

(222-235 A. D.) *Alexander Severus,* a lad of fourteen, was declared emperor by the praetorians and was accepted by the Senate. He was completely dominated by his mother, Julia

Mammaea. He had to face revolts in the provinces, and was slain in a mutiny while fighting the Gaul invaders in Germany, as was his mother. The mutiny was probably led by Maximinus Thrax, a Thracian legionnaire who became emperor.

Alexander Severus tried to reduce extravagance and taxes; he encouraged literature and the arts, and he preserved an open mind in religious matters. In his private chapel he had busts of Orpheus, Abraham, Apollonius of Tyana and Jesus Christ.

(235-238 A. D.) *Maximinus Thrax* was a shepherd of Thrace, whose immense strength attracted the attention of the Roman leaders. He entered the army and rose to be commander of the Fourth Legion in command of the army on the Rhine under Emperor Alexander Severus. The army proclaimed him emperor, and Alexander was murdered. Maximinus administered the provinces well, but took no interest in Italy, the Senate or the Roman populace. Revolts broke out in Africa under the Gordians.

The Senate declared the two Gordians, father and son who were serving in Carthage, Africa, as joint emperors and issued a decree against Maximinus. Gordian II, however, was killed in a battle at Carthage, and his father committeed suicide.

The Senate then declared two other military men co-emperors, Pupienus Maximus and Balbinus. Pupienus took the field of battle; Balbinus kept order in Rome. Maximinus marched toward Rome to take revenge on his enemies. He devastated the countryside as his army advanced, but the inhabitants of northern Italy resisted; they destroyed bridges, food and shelter. His soldiers revolted, and he was slain in his tent. It was Italy's early experience with a long series of barbaric invasions which were to follow during the next two centuries.

Pupienus Maximus and Balbinus were declared emperors. They were murdered the same year by the praetorians who forced their way into the palace while all the people were at the games.

(238-244 A. D.) *Gordian III,* the grandson of Gordian II, became sole emperor. He was under the control of his mother's eunuchs and his father-in-law, who persuaded him to lead the army against the Persians who had invaded the Roman province, Mesopotamia. Gordian opened the Temple of Jarius for the last recorded time and marched eastward. He drove the Persians out of Mesopotamia, but Philip the Arabian stirred discontent in the army, and Gordian III was murdered by mutinous soldiers.

(244-249 A. D.) *Philip* the Arab became emperor and his reign was distinguished by the celebration of the secular games, for only the fourth time since Augustus. They celebrated the one-thousandth anniversary of the foundation of Rome, a show of great magnificence, pomp, reverence and superstition. Philip was murdered in 249 A. D.

(249-251 A. D.) *Decius*—Gaius Messius—to whom Philip gave command of the army on the Danube, was proclaimed emperor against his will. Philip attacked him and was slain at Verona. Decius and his son fell in battle with the Goths. Priscus declared himself emperor under Gothic protection. Decius conducted a systematic persecution of the Christians and tried to restore the religion and institutions of ancient Rome.

(251-253 A. D.) *Gallus*—A brief reign.

(253-260 A. D.) *Valerian* with his son, Gallienus, was attacked on all sides by the barbarians, chiefly the able German Suevic tribes Alemanni. Gallienus married Pipa, daughter of a king of the Suevic tribe, and was resented by the Roman nobles. Valerian was taken prisoner by the Shah of Persia and disappeared from history (260 A. D.).

(260-268 A. D.) *Gallienus* deprived the senators of their commands. Pestilence ravaged the empire; the Goths ravaged the chief cities of Greece; his generals rebelled. His reign was called the reign of the Thirty Tyrants, and he was murdered by his own soldiers.

(268-270 A. D.) *Claudius II Gothicus*—Marcus Aurelius—was an able general who defeated the Alemanni and the Goths. Very popular, able and brave, he died of the plague.

(270-275 A. D.) *Aurelian*—Lucius Domitius—was born of humble parents in Pannonia. An able general, he was proclaimed emperor on the death of Claudius II, with approval of the soldiers. He defeated the Germans and Goths on the Rhine and the Danube; he defeated his pretenders to the throne; he led his army toward Persia and brought Zenobia, Queen of Palmyra, to a triumph in Rome. Then, he set out again to invade Persia and was murdered through the treachery of his secretary, Eros. He was the first emperor to wear the diadem and assumed the title of Lord and God on medals and is known in history as "Restorer of the Empire."

(275-276 A. D.) *Tacitus* (and Florianus 276 A. D.). There was a quick succession and procession of emperors in the ten-year period between 275 and 284 A. D. A few months after the assassination of Aurelian, the Senate chose Marcus Claudius Tacitus for the high office and he was accepted by the army. He claimed descent from the historian, Tacitus. A very wealthy man, he set in motion some reforms; however, he died in the field with his army in Cilicia after a victory over the Goths. The cause of death was stated to have been hardship and fatigue, but it was rumored that he was slain by his own soldiers. Tacitus reigned as emperor for six months and was succeeded by his brother.

(276 A. D.) *Florianus,* who was promptly put to death by his soldiers.

(276-282 A. D.) *Probus*—Marcus Aurelius—was an able and popular emperor and general. He quickly disposed of three usurpers, cleared the Germans out of Gaul, then in times of peace kept the soldiers at the peaceful occupations of planting vineyards, and draining marshes. They reacted by murdering him, though they repented later and built a monument to his memory.

(282-283 A. D.) *Carus*—Marcus Aurelius—succeeded Probus by proclamation of his soldiers. He punished the assassins of Probus but was suspected of being party to the plot, as he was prefect of the praetorian guard (our "secret service" whose duty was to protect the emperor). He took the field against the Persians in the Far East, leaving his elder son, Carinus, in charge at Rome and took the younger Numerianus on the expedition. Within the year, he died "suddenly" in the midst of military victories. (This was double talk for "murder by his soldiers.")

(283-284 A. D.) *Carinus* and *Numerianus*, the two sons of Carus, ruled briefly. Carinus set himself up in magnificent splendor and abandoned dissipation in Rome. Numerianus was forced by his army to be led back home, and he was murdered on the way. Diocletian was proclaimed emperor by the army. Carinus engaged him in battle for the throne, but was assassinated in the field.

(285-305 A. D.) *Diocletian* (286-305 A. D. Maximian). Marcus Diocletian was elected emperor by a group of officers, and he took office in 285 A. D. His first act was to murder, with his own hands, the prefect of the praetorians, Arrius Aper. He named one "Augustus" and two "Caesars" who ruled segments of the empire which he allotted to them—Maximian, Constantius Chlorus and Galerius. Diocletian destroyed the power of the Senate, and all traces of the republican institutions; he changed Rome into an absolute monarchy, using the full ceremonial of Eastern monarchs. He ruled Rome as a vast bureaucracy. It has been said that he "sacrificed the interests of the people to the preservation of the state."

Diocletian launched another cruel persecution of the Christians. He thought he could strengthen the empire by reviving the dying pagan religion, and he realized that the Christian faith of millions of his subjects stood in the path to that goal. Diocletian was smart enough to avoid the usual "sudden" death of emperors; he abdicated in 305 A. D. and retired to Salona where he lived quietly for several years.

(305-311 A. D.) *Galerius* at once assumed the title of Augustus with Constantius Chlorus and expected to become the sole ruler of Rome, upon his colleague's death. He failed, however, to take his colleague's son, Constantine, into his calculations for the future. Galerius appointed his friend Licinius "Augustus" which brought the total of his associated "Augusti" and "Caesars" to six. With all this help he devoted his life "to the enjoyment of pleasure . . ." In 305 A. D. he published an edict of persecution of the Christians. This cruel series lasted until 311 A. D. when he was forced by Licinius and Constantine to add his name to theirs on the general *Edict of Toleration for Christians,* thereby ending the pagan persecutions of the Christians.

(311-324 A. D.) *Constantine I* the Great and *Licinius.* Constantine was the son of the Roman emperor, Constantius Chlorus (the Pale) who ruled jointly with Galerius. In the distribution of territory to the associate Augusti, Constantius was given dominion over Gaul and Britain. He was a brave, able and gentle ruler who fell in battle against the Picts and Scots in 306 A. D. in England. His son, known as Constantine the Great, was born in Serbia in 288 A. D. His mother was Flavia Helena, whom St. Ambrose described as an innkeeper. (There has been some doubt that Constantius and Helena were married.)

Constantine, as a boy, was sent as a hostage to the eastern court and served under Galerius on the Danube. When his father became co-emperor with Galerius, he demanded his son's return. Galerius stalled and Constantine fled by night and prevented pursuit by taking all the horses with him. He joined his father who was about to cross to Britain to thwart an invasion of Picts and Scots. Constantius won the battle, which took place at York in 306 A. D., but lost his life. The army acclaimed his son, Constantine, as "Augustus." Constantine was reluctant, and patient; during the next six years, Maximian, Galerius, Diocletian, Maximinus Daia and Maxentius all plotted or fought against him. Meanwhile, Constantine searched for legal, rather than forceful, means for establishing himself as emperor.

In 311 A. D. Constantine I and Licinius became emperors of Rome. The Milan Edict of Toleration of Christians was issued by them in 312 A. D. Peace reigned for nine years, but Licinius resumed persecutions in 321 A. D.

Constantine and Licinius engaged in war in 324 A. D. and Licinius was defeated, captured and imprisoned. In 324 A. D. Constantine reigned alone as emperor of the Christian Roman Empire—thus the pagan Roman Empire was at an end.

5. ALARIC—GOTHIC CHIEF—AT THE CAPTURE OF ROME 410 A. D.

There is a legend, current in histories, of Alaric's capture of Rome which reveals how the Christian religion had moderated the instincts of the fierce Gothic barbarians. When the people of Rome knew they were about to be raided by the Goths, they tried to hide their valuables. (The people of Washington, D. C. reacted the same way on the day "General" Coxey was to lead "Coxey's Army" on their protest march to the Capitol. The author has a vivid memory, as a very small tot, that parents kept children indoors that day, and the owner of the peanut and candy stand at the corner of Pennsylvania Avenue and Eighteenth Street took all the boards of his stand down, carted them away and disappeared completely from the scene for as long as Coxey was in the city.)

In Rome, in 410 A. D., the day before Alaric would surely burst through the gates of that city at the head of his horde of barbarians, the people tried to hide their treasures. One elderly maiden lady's home was forced open by a Gothic captain who demanded all of her gold and silver. She showed him a rich store of plate and vessels so rare and beautiful that the Goth was fairly stunned. He prepared to cart it away, but she warned him that the treasures were not hers, but were the consecrated vessels from the altars of St. Peter's. The captain, halted by awe and reverence, sent to Alaric for instructions, whereupon the king replied immediately with an order to deliver them at once to St. Peter's.

The captain marched his soldiers in military formation through the streets of the city to the Vatican, as protection for a long procession of civilians and clergy who carried the consecrated vessels aloft. A multitude of Christians and pagans joined the procession and took safe sanctuary for themselves, also, in the Vatican.

St. Augustine's *City of God* deals—in part—with the pagan accusations that Christ and the Christians had angered the Roman gods, and Rome had been sacked to punish the people for turning from their idols to the Christian faith. St. Augustine, in his rejoinder, reminded the accusers of how their very own lives had been saved by taking sanctuary in a Christian church under the very protection of the Gothic army, in the wake of the holy sacramental vessels of the Church of St. Peter.

6. EMPERORS OF THE CHRISTIAN ROMAN EMPIRE FROM CONSTANTINE THE GREAT, 337 A. D., TO THE END OF THE EMPIRE IN THE WEST, 476 A. D.

(337-340 A. D.) *Constantine II, Constantius II, Constans I*. Constantine I, the Great, died on May 22, 337 A. D., at Nicomedia, after having received Christian baptism by Eusebius. He was buried in the Church of the Apostles in the city named for him, Constantinople. He was succeeded by three sons, Constantine II, Constans I and Constantius II who were designated by their father to succeed him. The army endeavored to massacre the rest of the family to insure the succession, but Julian and Gallus escaped. The elder Constantine II claimed control over the other two, but Constans did not submit. He was given Italy and Africa. Constantine II took Britain, Spain and Gaul. Constantius II took the eastern provinces. Constantine II invaded Italy and was killed in battle (340 A. D.).

(340-350 A. D.) *Constantius II* and *Constans I*. Constans was killed in the rebellion of Magnentius in 350 A. D. in the Pyrenees.

(350-351 A. D.) *Constantius II*. While making war against Shapur, Monarch of Persia, the revolt of Magnentius demanded his presence in the west, after Constans had been killed. He sent his cousin Gallus to Syria to carry on the war against Shapur and he went west to engage Magnentius in a bloody battle at Nursa on the Drave. He defeated Magnentius in 351 A. D. but the losses were so great on both sides that the Roman military forces were permanently weakened. The eastern and western empires were again united under one emperor, and Constantius II ruled in splendor, like the Persian monarch he had observed. In 355 A. D. he sent his cousin, Julian, as commander to Gaul. He visited Rome in 357 A. D., set up the obelisk—which he had brought from Heliopolis, in the Circus Maximus—moved the Altar of Victory to mark the end of paganism and, in 359 A. D., returned to his war in Asia against Shapur. He ordered Julian's army in Gaul to march east, but they revolted and proclaimed Julian as emperor. Constantius started to march west, but died on the way at Tarsus in 361 A. D. Historians say that he took his duties as head of the empire and head of the Church seriously, but that his mistake was to depend upon the unapproachable circle of palace officials of the oriental type of monarchy which Diocletian had established.

(361-363 A. D.) *Julian*, the Apostate, was born in Constantinople in 332 A. D., the nephew of Constantine the Great. He and his half brother, Gallus, had escaped from the efforts of the soldiers to exterminate all members of the family except the three sons of Constantine the Great. He was carefully educated under Christian bishops and rhetoricians. The philosophy and culture of the Hellenic world had a strong attraction for him, and he associated the Greek culture with the Greek pagan religion. Julian was liberated and went to Athens. But Constantius II needed him, so he was summoned to Milan, where the emperor bestowed upon him the hand of his sister, Helena, the title of Caesar and the government of the provinces of Gaul. Julian moved to Paris. His armies achieved great victories at Sens,

Strasburg and elsewhere, and Julian's administration of Gaul was successful.

He is remembered chiefly for his efforts to create a new pagan religion and to substitute it for the official Christian faith. However, he was mortally wounded in the war with the Persians, which he had inherited from Constantius II, and died in 363 A. D. Julian was a rare combination of general, statesman, culture and character.

(363-364 A. D.) *Jovian* was born in 351 A. D. and served as emperor for only eight months. He died on his return from the war in Persia in which he served Julian as captain of the imperial bodyguard. He was unexpectedly proclaimed emperor when Julian died and established Christianity as the state religion. He reinstated Athanasius as archbishop of Alexandria.

(364-375 A. D.) *Valentinian* I (the Great) and *Valens,* with *Gratian* from 367 A. D. He was an officer of the guard with Jovian and was chosen emperor by army officers at Nicaea upon Jovian's death. He named his younger brother, Valens, as co-emperor. Valentinian took charge of the empire in the west, with his headquarters at Milan, Paris, Rheims. His chief duties were to guard the western frontiers against the Picts, Scots, Saxons, Burgundians and Alemanni. This he did well with the aid of his general, Theodosius. He died in a fit of apoplexy on the Danube in 375 A. D. Valentinian was a member of the Christian Church, a founder of schools and a friend of the poor.

(375-378 A. D.) *Valens,* born in 328 A. D., served as emperor in the east. After making war against the Persians, the Huns swarmed in from the east upon the Goths who asked the emperor for permission to cross the Danube. He granted it under certain conditions, which the Goths declared his generals violated. The Goths attacked the Roman army and in 378 A. D. annihilated the army with cruel slaughter at Adrianople. Valens perished with his army in 378 A. D.; the Goths no longer feared Roman military might. Valens launched a unique persecution, one against magicians.

(378-383 A. D.) *Gratian,* son of Valentinian I, born in 359 A. D., now took over the head of the empire. He was young and ceded military duties to General Theodosius. During his reign Gratian prohibited pagan worship in Rome, and abolished many privileges of pagans. He also refused to wear the insignia of the Pontifex Maximus, as unbefitting a Christian. A revolt against him was raised in Britain, because of his indolent life. After appearing in public in Paris in frivolous garb, his soldiers deserted him; he fled to Lyons where he was delivered over to a rebel general by the governor, and was assassinated.

(378-392 A. D.) *Valentinian II* was the younger half brother of Gratian. He became emperor at the age of fourteen, though his mother, Justine, was the ruler. Making their home in Milan, the rebel from Britain, Magnus Maximus, pursued them there, causing them to flee to Theodosius, emperor of the east, who restored Valentinian to this throne in 388 A. D., only to be murdered in Gaul in 392 A. D.

(378-395 A. D.) *Theodosius* the Great was the son of Valentinian's great general and was born in Spain in 346 A. D. After the battle of Adrianople (378 A. D.) Gratian divided the empire, Theodosius taking all the eastern provinces under his command. He waged wars successfully against the Visigoths under Fritigern and the Ostrogoths under Alatheus. A skillful diplomat, he persuaded the Visigoth king Athanasius to join his forces, and provided 40,000 of his people with land for settlement. After celebrating a triumph in Rome in 389 A. D. he remained there for some years enjoying a life of gluttony and pleasure. After a final victorious battle against enemies in Italy, he named his two sons, Arcadius and Honorius, his successors and succumbed to the ravages of dropsy in 395 A. D.

The Roman Empire (395 A. D.) was permanently partitioned between east and west. The following emperors reigned only in the *west:*

(395-423 A. D.) *Honorius,* son of Theodosius I, born 383 A. D.

became emperor of the west in 395 A. D. He was attacked on all sides by barbarians. Italy was saved by his guardian and father-in-law, Stilicho, a Vandal chieftain. Gaul was overrun and Britain was abandoned in 409 A. D.; Stilicho was murdered in 409 A. D.; Alaric, the Visigoth, invaded Italy and sacked Rome; Honorius made peace with Alaric's successor, Adolphus (412 A. D.) who married Honorius' sister, Placidia, and removed his troops to Gaul.

Honorius was a diligent supporter of the Christian Church and equally diligent in suppressing pagan worship. He prohibited the pagan ceremonies in 399 A. D., and the revenues of the pagan temples were confiscated and used to support the army; he abolished the gladiatorial shows, reduced taxes and improved the administration of justice. When Italy was invaded, he moved to Ravenna, where he died in 423 A. D.

(425-455 A. D.) *Valentinian* III, born in 419 A. D., the son of Constantius and Placidia, became emperor of the west at the age of six. The western empire suffered great losses in his reign. The Vandals conquered the province of Africa; large sections of Spain and Gaul were appropriated by the barbarians; Genseric raided Sicily and other coastal areas.

His general, Aetius, gained a great victory over Attila in France in 451 A. D., but Attila ravaged northern Italy the following year. Valentinian murdered Aetius in 454 A. D. and, in turn, was murdered in 455 A. D. by barbarian companions of Aetius. History rates Valentinian III as selfish and vindictive.

(455 A. D.) *Petronius Maximus* reigned only three months after the death of his one-time close friend, Valentinian III. This friendship turned quickly into bitter hatred when the emperor committed an indignity upon Petronius' wife. He was murdered by barbarian mercenaries while he was trying to escape from the Vandals of Genseric who had landed at the mouth of the Tiber on their way to sack Rome.

(455-456 A. D.) *Avitus*. Information not available. Deposed.

(457-461 A. D.) *Majorian* was declared emperor by the regent after Avitus was deposed. He was an able general, and all his genius was needed to repel attacks by Vandals and other barbarians upon Compania, Africa and Spain. Majorian was forced to resign after a mutiny that was probably provoked by the regent, Ricimer. He was the author of some of the laws which are in the Theodosian Code—one forbade the practice of contractors to quarry their materials for new buildings out of the ancient monuments, such as the amphitheater, forum, etc.

Gibbon praises Majorian as an emperor whose virtues and devotion to his people were of high order. Gibbon believes the moral standards of his people had been so corrupted that they were not worthy of Majorian. The western empire was soon to fall of its own decay.

(461-465 A. D.) *Libius Severus* was nominally emperor for the next four years, but the regent, Ricimer, actually ruled.

(461-471 A. D.) Regent, *Ricimer,* was the son of barbarians, a prince of the Suevi and a princess of the Visigoths. As a youth he was a member of the court of Valentinian III, and rendered brilliant military service. He was authorized by the Senate to make war upon Avitus, whom he deposed. By then he was so powerful that he could select the next emperor, Majorian. But when Majorian took over rule in his own right, Ricimer forced him to abdicate and then arranged for his death by poison. Ricimer then placed Libius Severus upon the throne, but again employed poison to terminate his rule. For two years (465-467 A. D.) Ricimer, the emperor-maker, ruled without an emperor.

(467-472 A. D.) *Anthemius,* an able general, was the candidate of Leo I, as Roman emperor in the east, and was accepted by Ricimer. Soon, however, Ricimer was in a mood to declare war on Anthemius; but a truce was patched up by the bishop of Milan. In 472 A. D. Ricimer moved on Rome, proclaimed Olybrius as emperor and besieged and sacked Rome. Anthemius was massacred; Ricimer died, but in bed, of malignant fever.

(472 A. D.) *Olybrius* was sent by Leo to assist Anthemius against

his son-in-law, Ricimer. Upon the murder of his rival, Olybrius was proclaimed emperor. He lasted in that office for three months.

(473-475 A. D.) *Glycerius* and *Julius Nepos* chased each other into and out of the office of emperor for two years. Each was assassinated.

(475-476 A. D.) *Romulus Augustulus.* This brings us to the inglorious end of the Roman Empire in the west! Curiously, the name of the last emperor was the name of Rome's first king, Romulus, and Rome's first emperor, Augustus. But the fourteen-year-old lad had no other qualifications. The real ruler was the arch politician, Orestes, his father.

In 476 A. D. a captain of barbarian mercenaries in the employ of the empire, Odoacer, demanded that they should be given one-third of all the land in Italy. Orestes refused and was beheaded, but the boy was spared.

Odoacer sent word to the emperor of the east, Zeno, that the Roman Empire of the west was ended. Odoacer, an Arian Christian, made himself king of Italy. For fourteen years the Gothic kingdom of Italy managed as well or better than had many of the previous Roman rulers. In 490 A. D. Odoacer was overthrown by the king of the Ostrogoths, Theodoric, who initiated an age of government, peace and prosperity. Gibbon says of Theodoric, ". . . whose name excites and deserves the attention of mankind."

7. FOUNDING OF ISLAM AND EFFORTS TO PENETRATE WESTERN CIVILIZATION (7TH-13TH CENTURIES)

It is interesting that three great world religions originated in the area between the Tigris River and the Mediterranean Sea; that each of the three worshiped one God only; each taught its followers the virtue and practice of charity.

These are: the Jewish religion, whose recorded history goes back 4,000 years; the Christian religion, founded by Jesus and his disciples who were practicing Jews in 30 A. D. at Jerusalem,

Palestine; and the Mohammedan or Islam religion founded at Mecca, Arabia, a few years prior to 616 A. D.

Mohammedanism-Islam

Mohammed was a native of Arabia, a conductor of caravans across the wide deserts, a thoughtful and wise man, who absorbed information from all the travelers whom he met on his caravan journeys, and who heard God speaking to him in the silences, revealing eternal laws and truths which he recorded in the Koran.

These revelations were made to him in secret, and he was not permitted to discuss them except with his wife and family. Consequently, it was not until 616 A. D. that he was allowed to preach his message publicly, which he did in Mecca. Calling his religion Islam, he proclaimed one God only, Allah; he himself was Allah's prophet on Earth.

Mohammed knew of Abraham and the other Jewish prophets and writings. He also knew of Jesus and he had respect for them all.

Islam had a swift growth. In 628 A. D. Mohammed wrote to all the rulers on Earth and announced the revelations which he had received from God. His missionaries evangelized the other Arabian nations promptly and thoroughly; and his symbol, the crescent, began to contend vigorously for the souls of men with the cross, the symbol of the Christians.

Islam made efforts to penetrate Western civilization—youthful Europe—in the seventh, eighth, ninth, eleventh and twelfth centuries. Had Islam succeeded, Western civilization would have resulted in a different culture. The result was the counterattacks which the Christian crusades made upon Islam in the eleventh, twelfth, and thirteenth centuries.

Encounter in Western Europe Between Christians and Islam

In the seventh century A. D. the Arab Mohammedans invaded Algeria and Morocco and swept the Berbers into wars to conquer all North Africa and even beyond the Strait of Gibraltar.

They established themselves in Spain for centuries, building the beautiful mosques which still stand. The Alhambra, a palace and fortress of the Moorish monarchs of Granada built in 1248 A. D., is the most famous reminder of Islam's invasion of Europe.

But the Moslems were not satisfied with their European conquest in Spain, so they set their course toward Rome, and their army started its eastern march from Spain toward the Holy City (730 A. D.). The Saracens, as these invaders were then called, progressed steadily, while the city and the church were being assailed from the other side by the barbarous Lombards.

At this time a capable family in France (which was loyal to the Christian Church and the papacy) was appealed to by the Pope for military help. A response came from a member of this family, Charles Martel, who encountered the Saracens in battle at Poitiers in France. He utterly defeated them and broke their spirit as well, sending the Saracens retreating behind the Pyrenees. The Moslem faith prospered in parts of Spain, but Rome and the Christian Church were preserved.

It was Charles Martel's son, Pepin, who was chosen king of the Franks, with the help of Pope Zachary, and was crowned at Soissons in 752 A. D. And it was Pepin's son, and Charles Martel's grandson, who was crowned in 800 A. D. by Pope Leo III as the first emperor of the Holy Roman Empire—Charlemagne the Great.

Later Encounters of the Christians and Moslems

Representatives of these two religions—Christianity and Islam—had dramatic and bloody encounters during the following 500 years.

The first of these three dramatic meetings was in eastern Europe, over 600 years after the early Christian Church had been founded in Greece and the adjoining European countries.

The Moslems first tried in 672 A. D. and again in 717 A. D. to establish themselves in eastern Europe, but did not succeed at that time. Their effort in the east was against Constantinople, seat of the Byzantine Christian Church, but Constantinople repulsed them.

They made another effort in 800 A. D., this time via diplomacy aimed at the Bulgarians who, originally a Turkish people, had conquered most of the Balkan peninsula in 810 A. D. under their Prince Krum (he who used the skull of the defeated Byzantine emperor, Nicephorus, as his drinking cup). They were a pagan people, and for some time they wavered between adopting the Christian or the Moslem faith. Then King Boris married a Byzantine princess and moved himself and his people over to the Christian faith in 852 A. D.

But 200 years later, the Islam religion was brought into the Balkans by the Ottoman Turks after their victorious armies had crossed the Bosphorus. They found the people of Macedonia, Epirus, Illysia, Yugo-Slavia and Bulgaria Christians, but they converted all they could to Islam. They disarmed the rest and conferred upon them the privilege of paying taxes to the Ottoman empire, which included Hungary and Roumania. They also imposed upon them a levy of 1,000 Christian youths per year for their standing military force, the Janisaries.

Many Moslems are still to be found today in the mountains of Albania, long known as Montenegro.

The Third Encounter Between Christians and Moslems

The third historic clash between Christians and Islam occurred in the eleventh and twelfth centuries, in Palestine rather than in Europe. Consequently, the issues of these encounters did not have the same influence upon the direction and the character of Western civilization as did the two previous encounters in Europe. If Islam had been successful in either of these two earlier efforts to overthrow the European Christian Church, they probably would have brought about the same sort of civilization in Europe which they created in western North Africa. The Christian civilization of western North Africa, or Roman Africa, which missionaries from Rome, including their greatest leader, St. Augustine, had established, was regarded as

a model for other Christian communities—peaceful, friendly,
prosperous, generous. This was western North Africa of the first
seven centuries. Then came the invasion of that land by Moslem Arabs—and Christianity was displaced.

8. THE CHRISTIAN CRUSADES TO FREE JERUSALEM
   FROM MOHAMMEDANISM

   The third historic spectacular clash between Christians and
Islam was in Palestine. It was in the form of the famous crusades, in the eleventh and twelfth centuries. These were the
organized marches by European Christians on Jerusalem and
Palestine for the purpose of taking away from the Moslems,
who were then in possession of the Holy Land, the sacred
places connected with the birth, life and death of Jesus.

   Since the author has a rather guilty feeling that the shining
crusaders were galloping backward on the path of civilization,
instead of forward toward our west, the following about the
Christian crusades will suffice:

   The first crusade was launched in 1096 by Pope Urban II,
who called for volunteers to "take the cross" and march on
Jerusalem to rescue Jesus' sepulchre from Islam (Seljuk Turk
Moslems). Thousands responded. The first wave of common
folks under Peter the Hermit went by land, only to become a
pile of whitened bones outside of Constantinople before the
second wave of knights, princes and their paid attendants arrived by boat—150,000 in number, finally entering Jerusalem
in 1099 after a terrible slaughter.

   1149—The second crusade was organized by Pope Eugenius
III in response to a call for help from the Franks in Antioch,
where followers of Jesus were first called "Christians." It ended
in complete failure.

   1187—Saladin, Moslem military genius, organized a counter-
crusade and recaptured Jerusalem. He threw the Franks and
Romans out of the areas they had ruled for nearly a century.

   1189—The third crusade was called to rescue the holy sepulchre again from defilement by the Moslems. It was dominated

by the kings of Germany, France and England. They granted freedom from taxes (Saladin tithe) and from payment of interest on debts to those who would "take the cross." It ended in politicians' quarrels between the generals, and agreements negotiated by diplomats.

1202—The fourth crusade was first directed against Egypt, because Moslem power was then centered there. But the politicians of Venice got into the act because, no doubt, of their trade with Egypt; and the crusade finally attacked and captured the Turkish city of Constantinople. It is generally judged that this crusade was a disaster for the papacy at Rome and for future crusades.

1212—*The Children's Crusade* was pathetic and tragic and should have ended all crusades, but instead it was used to try to revive further crusading zeal. The Pope wrote, "The very children put us to shame."

A shepherd boy of France, named Stephen, induced thousands of children to follow him as he rode on a wagon to Marseille. He told the army of boys he would lead them dry-shod over the seas to the Holy Land, but his army was kidnapped, and the boys were sold into slavery in Egypt. In Cologne, Germany, a child named Nicholas recruited 20,000 children crusaders with similar promises and led them into Italy. These children disappeared from sight beyond a curtain of silence; their pitiable crusade left nothing behind it to show except the later legend of the Pied Piper of Hamelin.

Other crusades were:

1215—The fifth crusade
1228—The sixth crusade
1245—The seventh crusade
1267—The eighth crusade

In the Wake of the Crusades

For the next 100 years others dreamed and talked of mounting new crusades, but none materialized from the ghost of these strange demonstrations of zeal and emotional yearning for glory. There can not be the slightest doubt that the crusades had a profound effect upon the commercial development of the West, and the East as well.

But one who is concerned with tracing the finer impulses and motivations of civilized man toward a society with the characteristics of freedom and goodwill can only wish that the spiritual forces which flowed westward from Galilee had not been buffeted and betrayed by the bloody and prideful crusades which swept eastward for two crucial centuries with the goal of capturing the sepulchre of the gentle Man of Galilee who had first released the nobler impulses of Western civilization.

9. ORDERS OF MENDICANT FRIARS (1200-1300 A. D.)

The four great Orders of Mendicant Friars, and several lesser orders, came into being in the thirteenth century; all were in response to deeply felt needs of the changing times.

The social phenomenon which created the need for these new agencies of spiritual and material service was the shift of populations from the rural life to heavily concentrated city life.

Up to the eleventh and twelfth centuries the settled nations of Europe and England were organized on the feudal system of large landlords—feudal barons. Then began the shift to towns and cities, and the traditional parish system of the Church was not able to minister to the people who gathered in these centers. The destitute and poor were pushed, as usual, into crowded sections of the cities and the parochial clergy did not know how to meet their spiritual and human needs.

St. Francis and St. Dominic sensed the need and each gathered around him an order of Friars with the oath of austerity, poverty and the return to the simple life of Jesus and His apostles. The Augustinian Black Friars and the Carmelite White Friars adopted similar rules.

Within a short period of time they had spread all over Europe and into Asia and other sections of the world. Their friars were numbered in the tens of thousands; their friaries were established in all the cities of western Europe and theological chairs in the universities were held by Dominicans and Franciscans.

1. *The Franciscans*—This order of Mendicant Friars, probably the most effective of all, was founded by Francis (1182-1226) the son of a well-to-do merchant of Assisi, Italy. He lived a gay life as a youth, and spent his father's money with enthusiasm until the age of twenty.

He then became conscience-stricken by the contrast between his own life of comfort and the sad lives of the poor all about him. He withdrew from his wealthy companions and began to make friends with the destitute and disabled.

When his father threatened to punish him by disinheritance, Francis willingly gave up his claim on his father's estate; he even took off the fine clothes, put on some old garments and began the life of a hermit. But this solitary life did not satisfy his desire to serve the poor and the friendless, so he began to tell others of his concern, and soon a dozen or so rich young friends joined him. They left their riches and luxuries behind them and the group walked about Italy joyously preaching the simple Gospel of Jesus.

Francis appealed to the Pope for approval which was reluctantly granted. Before long they were formed into an order, and they sent missionaries into all of Central and western Europe and to the British Isles. Francis, himself, feared that this would lead his followers ultimately to abandon the simple life, and that the order would become rich, which it did after his death. He clearly stated his own purpose in a letter: "I, little brother Francis, desire to follow the life and the poverty of Jesus Christ, persevering therein until the end; and I beg you all and exhort you to persevere in this most holy life of poverty, and take good care never never to depart from it upon the advice and teachings of any one whomsoever."

The Franciscan Order of Mendicant Friars was founded on Francis' sincere love for poor and lowly people, and he won from the people a love and reverence that remains in the hearts of Western man to this day.

2. *The Dominican Order of Mendicant Friars*—The founder of the Dominican Order, St. Dominic, had a different vocation for the creation of his equally influential order. Dominic (1170-1221) was born in Spain and, unlike St. Francis, was a trained priest. He made a visit with his bishop to Toulouse in southern France and was greatly shocked to observe the strange heresy of the Albigensians, who were preaching their belief in two Gods: the God of Good and the God of Evil. They declared that these two powerful Gods were contending with each other for the souls of men. Dominic argued with these preachers by day and night, but could not change their beliefs, so he resolved to dedicate the rest of his life to fighting heresy.

Emperor Frederick II, who was a very aggressive leader of that era and who engaged in bitter controversies with other leaders of state and church, tried to suppress the heresy by force. In 1208 Pope Innocent III called upon Christian princes for armies to join in the fight on the heretical Albigensians, and southern France was devastated by a blood-thirsty war for the next seven years.

In 1214 Dominic and his followers proposed to go out into the world on a preaching mission and asked the Pope for approval of a new order. Approval was given; the Dominican Order of Mendicant Friars was founded and by 1221 had sixty friaries in Europe and the British Isles. They were called the "Preaching Friars," but they were especially interested in education, as scholars and teachers. Two noted Dominican educators were Albert Magnus and Thomas Aquinas.

3. *The Carmelites* originated about 1150. This order of Mendicant Friars was started by a crusader, Berthold, whose company was defeated in its attacks on the Moslems in Palestine. He and ten companions are said to have taken up their abode in or near "the cave of Elias" on Mount Carmel, north of the Sea of Galilee. They lived there as hermits until they migrated to Cypress, Sicily, France and England. They became an Order of Mendicant Friars in 1247, and about 100 years later St. Teresa founded a Carmelite convent. In 1600 the Carmelites

split into two orders. There are now about 2,000 members of the order (known as White Friars) spread over Europe, Spanish America and the British Isles.

4.   *The Augustinian Order of Hermits or Friars* was organized about 1250. This fourth Order of Mendicant Friars was created through the merger of several small congregations of hermits into a single religious order. This action was taken by the popes of the period who gave the united society the name "Augustinian Order of Hermits or Friars."

This order adopted the "Rule of St. Augustine" which the great fourth century scholar had written centuries previously in a letter of advice to a community of nuns as to their daily life.

There was an undercurrent of unrest stirring in several sections of the Christian Church during this period of the early years of the Orders of Mendicant Friars. They were moving about in Europe and England getting close to the common people and sharing their needs and thoughts and frustrations.

Is it possible that the Mendicant Friars themselves were, unconsciously, in revolt? Were they giving witness in their own lives of poverty to their dissatisfaction with the formal message of the Christian faith? They were good and faithful children of the Church, but their very efforts to establish new channels for bringing the Gospel to the common people may have helped to raise doubts as to the efficacy of the older established channels.

There was a longing in many hearts for a warmer relationship between the individual and his God. The Mendicant Friars stimulated that longing as they wandered about the Western world and preached and taught their own simple version of the Gospel of Christ.

It was an Augustinian monk who ignited the spark which set the Reformation ablaze in Germany—Martin Luther. The Mendicant Friars—in Luther's action—may have helped to create a force of far-reaching importance in the history of Western man.

The effect of Luther's act, himself an Augustinian monk, was also far-reaching as it related to the Augustinian order. The

German congregations of the order were dissolved and many of the other houses of the Augustinian order did not survive the Reformation. It is said that there are about 100 Augustinian congregations remaining now, chiefly in Europe, America and Ireland.

10. The Manufacture of Books, and the Rise of Public Opinion

Western man slowly, but inevitably it would seem, appropriated from much older civilizations certain media for the communication of ideas, and created *de novo* certain other media for that essential use. These media were paper, movable type, the printing press and the book bindery.

Until all of these essential factors were brought together by Western man in the fifteenth century, it was not possible to distribute ideas or ideals via the written word to all the people. Nor was it possible to make use of the written word to develop a fully informed public opinion on any great issue related to the general well-being of mankind.

Paper: The Chinese invented the art of making paper, probably about 200 B. C. The Arabs engaged the invading Chinese at Samarkand about 751 A. D. and among their captives were certain prisoners who were skilled in paper-making. The Arabs learned the art from them and soon were using paper made from linen for their official manuscripts. Other materials were also used by the Arabs: flax, rags, vegetable fibres.

Soon it was imported into Europe, and the Moors began (in the twelfth century) to manufacture paper in Spain and Italy, and then in Germany and England.

Before paper: Until the introduction of paper in Europe, there was no mass distribution of manuscripts of any branch of learning. Paper was essential to the general distribution of information and knowledge and opinion.

Before paper, a manuscript was written on a continuous roll of parchment or vellum and then rolled up for safekeeping or to be passed on to another reader.

When paper was first used in Europe, the manuscript was written on single sheets, folded once, then collected in sections of convenient size and held together by stitches through the center fold. Wooden boards or leather-hide covers were added. These volumes were still produced in very small quantities, of course, until the invention of movable type and the printing press. They never reached large numbers of the people, which suited most rulers very nicely.

If a volume was intended for the use of a V. I. P., the covers were richly ornamented and decorated, even with valuable gems and golden bands. Gem-incrusted Bibles were among the treasures which the marauding Danes sought when they ran their viking ship into the estuaries of Ireland, England and mid-Europe to sack the monasteries and churches located there.

The printing press: The invention of the first printing press was by Coster in 1446, or by Gutenberg in 1454. Printing of books changed promptly from an art to a business.

Many printing presses were set up quite promptly. One of the most famous was under the ownership of Aldus (at Venice, in 1495) who brought the famous scholar Erasmus to Venice to oversee the publication of a new edition of his *Adagia*. Aldus also printed and sold many Greek classics in small inexpensive volumes.

Basle, Switzerland, also became an active publishing city under the initiative of Froben (in 1468) who published the works of St. Jerome, Tertullian, St. Ambrose, etc. He also induced Erasmus to make residence at Basle for some years to edit and supervise the publication of his works.

A printing plant was set up in Paris, near the Sorbonne in 1470; and, in England, William Caxton established a printing business in 1476 at Westminster.

Informed public opinion: This was an essential forward move in the progress of Western civilization. New ideas of the worth and freedom of the individual were stirring the mind and conscience of Western man. He was restless—but scarcely knew why, or from what. Without printed journals and books the liberating ideas in the minds of men who were reaching for the basis of a better life would have found lodgment in only a small fraction of the growing numbers of restless men.

The distribution of printed books warranted H. G. Wells to write: ". . . the intellectual life of the world entered upon a new and far more vigorous phase. It ceased to be a little trickle from mind to mind; it became a broad flood in which thousands and presently scores and hundreds of thousands of minds participated."

Two books: Fully aware of the risk in selecting two books as illustrative of the effect of the newly created business of printing on the rise of public opinion, the following are suggested:

Utopia, by Sir Thomas More, 1510.

Sir Thomas More was born in London in 1478 and attended St. Anthony's School and then Christ College at Oxford. His father urged him to a career in law, but he drew back. He enjoyed his life at Oxford. He became a warm friend of Erasmus, preferred the life of a scholar, but was drawn into political life, during the reign of Henry VIII. The king made him Lord Chancellor and coveted his close friendship; but More had his own preferences and ideals. Refusing to approve Henry's divorce, and the king's break with Rome, he absented himself from the coronation of Anne Boleyn, and was marked for vengeance. Consequently, he was imprisoned in the Tower in 1535, was tried for treason and was beheaded; and his head was set up on the London Bridge. More was canonized by Pope Pius XI 400 years later.

Utopia, which Sir Thomas published in Latin in 1516, began a wide circulation in the English language in 1551. It was a witty satire on the English government and society of that period, and remains in many current lists of English classics.

Utopia was the narrative of a mariner who, having sailed the seven seas, described the fictitious Isle of Utopia and compared its pleasant society with the wretchedness of the poor and the luxury of the rich of England. It was reminiscent of Plato's

Republic and of St. Augustine's *City of God*. It gave a strong impetus to the rising desire for justice and freedom.

Pilgrim's Progress, by John Bunyan, 1678.

John Bunyan was born at Enslow, England, in 1628, the son of a tinker, a non-conformist, a Puritan.

Pilgrim's Progress was first published in 1678. Within only eight years, it went into ten editions. It was the allegorical story of the passage of a pilgrim—Mr. Christian—through life. The pilgrim passed through swamps and pleasant fields, up hill and down hill, through village and city and forests, but in a straight and narrow path which finally led him to the Shining Gate.

At first the book was published on the cheapest paper for servants and cottagers, the common people, but before long it was approved and read widely by the educated public as well.

The central character, Mr. Christian, loved God and followed faithfully his namesake, Christ Jesus. He was a shining example of Jesus' message of charity, of generosity, of love for fellowmen, of zeal for a better world on Earth.

BIBLIOGRAPHY

American Association of Fund-Raising Counsel, *Giving U.S.A.* (Annual).

Andrews, F. Emerson, *The Foundation Directory* (2nd ed.). New York: Russell Sage Foundation, 1964.

————, *Philanthropic Giving*. New York: Russell Sage Foundation, 1950.

Artz, Frederick B., *The Mind of the Middle Ages:* A. D. *200-1500* (2nd ed.). New York: Alfred A. Knopf, Inc., 1958.

Augustine, Saint, *The City of God,* abridged and translated by J. C. Wand. New York: Oxford University Press, 1963.

Bihlmeyer, Karl, *Church History,* Vol I, *Christian Antiquity*. Westminster, Md.: The Newman Press, 1958.

Boyd, William K., *The Ecclesiastical Edicts of the Theodosian Code*. New York: The Columbia University Press, 1905.

Cantor, Norman F., *Medieval History*. New York: The Macmillan Company, 1963.

Case, Shirley Jackson, *The Social Triumph of the Ancient Church*. New York: Harper & Brothers, Publishers, 1933.

Cheyney, Edward P., *The Dawn of a New Era: 1250-1453* A. D. New York: Harper & Brothers, Publishers, 1936.

Davies, A. Powell, *The Meaning of the Dead Sea Scrolls*. New York: The New American Library, 1956.

de Tocqueville, Alexis D., *Democracy in America* (2 vols.). New York: Schocken Books, Inc., 1961.

Durant, Will, *The Story of Civilization, Caesar and Christ*. New York: Simon and Schuster, Inc., 1944.

Fosdick, Raymond B., *John D. Rockefeller, Jr.* New York: Harper & Brothers, Publishers, 1956.

Gibbon, Edward, *The Decline and Fall of the Roman Empire*, D. M. Low, ed. New York: The Washington Square Press, Inc., 1962.

Goodspeed, Edgar J., *How to Read the Bible*. New York: Holt, Rinehart & Winston, Inc., 1946.

Hamilton, Edith, *The Roman Way*. New York: W. W. Norton & Company, Inc., 1932.

Harnack, Adolph, *The Mission and Expansion of Christianity in the First Three Centuries*. New York: Harper & Row, Publishers, 1962.

Haskins, Charles Homer, *The Renaissance of the 12th Century*. New York and Cleveland: World Publishing Company, 1957.

Heer, Frederich, *The Medieval World: Europe 1100-1350*. New York: New American Library, 1962.

Jordan, W. K., *Philanthropy in England: 1480-1660*. New York: Russell Sage Foundation, 1959.

———, *The Charities of Rural England: 1480-1660*. New York: Russell Sage Foundation, 1961.

Keyes, Nelson B., *The Story of the Bible World*. Maplewood, N. J.: C. S. Hammond & Co., Inc., 1958.

Latourette, Kenneth S., *History of the Expansion of Christianity* (Vol I), *The First Five Centuries*. New York: Harper & Brothers, Publishers, 1937.

———, *History of the Expansion of Christianity* (Vol II), *The 1000 Years of Uncertainty: 500-1500* A. D. New York: Harper & Brothers, Publishers, 1938.

Lecky, W. E. H., *The History of European Morals*. New York: George Braziller, Inc., 1955.

Marts, Arnaud C., *Philanthropy's Role in Civilization*. New York: Harper & Brothers, Publishers, 1953.

———, *Man's Concern for His Fellow Man*. New York: Marts & Lundy Incorporated, 1961.

Muller, Herbert J., *The Loom of History*. New York: Harper & Brothers, Publishers, 1958.

National Association of Social Workers, *Social Work Year Book*. New York: Russell Sage Foundation.

Probst, George E., ed., *The Happy Republic: A Reader in de Tocqueville's America*. New York: Harper & Brothers, Publishers, 1962.

Reinach, Salomon, *Orpheus: A History of Religions*. New York: Liveright Publishing Corp., 1962.

Smyth, J. Paterson, *How We Got Our Bible*. New York: Harper & Brothers, Publishers, 1894.

Stead, Francis Herbert, *The Story of Social Christianity* (2 Vols.). Jas. Clarke & Co., I.td., 1924.

Stevenson, J., ed. *New Eusebius*. New York: The Seabury Press, Inc., 1963.

Toynbee, Arnold J., *America and the World Revolution*. New York: Oxford University Press, 1962.

————, *Greek Civilization and Character*. New York: New American Library, 1954.

————, *The Historical Approach to Religion*. New York: Oxford University Press, 1956.

Uhlhorn, G., *Christian Charity in the Ancient Church,* trans. by Sophia Taylor. Edinburgh: T. & T. Clark, 1883.

Van Loon, Hendrik Willem, *The Arts*. New York: Simon & Schuster, Inc., 1937.

Wells, H. G., *The Outline of History*. New York: The Macmillan Company, 1921.

INDEX

231

ABOUT THE AUTHOR

Arnaud C. Marts was born in the parsonage of the Congregational Church in 1888, in the small village of Reeds Corner, Canandaigua County, New York. His parents were the Reverend William G. Marts and Irene Cartwright Marts. He graduated from East Aurora High School, and in 1910 from Oberlin College, Ohio, with Phi Beta Kappa honors.

After graduation from Oberlin, Marts's first job was as Boys' Work Secretary of the Y.M.C.A. at Pittsburgh, Pennsylvania. He then served as vice-president of the Standard Life Insurance Company, and in 1919, moved to New York City where he became one of the seven founding partners of the well-known fund counseling firm of Ward, Hill, Pierce and Wells.

In 1926 he withdrew from this firm and with George E. Lundy established their own firm of fund-counselors, Marts & Lundy, Inc., which has become one of the largest and most respected firms in the field. Arnaud Marts and George Lundy, and their staff of fifty associates, have counseled many thousands of religious, educational and philanthropic institutions which have received generous gifts totaling billions of dollars. Marts served as president of the company for thirty years, when he became chairman of the board.

It is Dr. Marts's career in this profession which has qualified him so uniquely to write this story of private generosity for the public good by which successive generations of Western man were able to pioneer each step of their progress toward a better world for all mankind.

During his whole career Dr. Marts has also been an active volunteer worker in a score of educational, religious and philanthropic causes. A sampling of them will suffice as evidence. For ten years he served as the part-time president of Bucknell University because a petition signed by all the students and faculty members of the college asked him to do so. For thirty years he served on the board of The American Leprosy Mission as director, vice-president, president, chairman of the board successively. For twenty years he has served as vice-chairman of the board of Wilkes College of which he was a founder; for five years he was president of the trustees of Woods Hole Oceanographic Institution. He has also served as a trustee of Oberlin College, Bradford Junior College, Geisinger Hospital. He was one of the founders of the American Association of Fund-Raising Counsel, and was its president for three terms. He serves on the Consistory of the Dutch Reformed Collegiate Church. He is a member of the Marble Collegiate Church.

Prior to World War II—1940-1941—he served at Harrisburg in the cabinets of Governor Arthur H. James and Governor Edward Martin in charge of Civilian Defense. In 1942 he was commissioned as Captain in the United States Coast Guard Reserve to become chief of the Temporary Reserve Division, for which he received the Navy Commendation Medal and Ribbon.

He is the author of two other books—*Philanthropy's Role in Civilization,* and *Man's Concern for His Fellow Man.* His articles in journals, and his addresses, have achieved a total circulation, directly and by requisition, of over a million copies.

It is interesting to observe, since Dr. Marts's book deals with Western civilization in Europe and America, that his ancestry is rooted in several of the basic strains of Western man.

His earliest maternal ancestor in America arrived by clipper from England at New Haven, Connecticut, in 1630, where he laid out a farm—part of which later became the campus of Yale University.

The author's first paternal ancestor in America arrived by boat from Germany at the mouth of the Delaware River about 1730 and sailed up the river where he laid out a farm in Northampton County, Pennsylvania.

Honorary degrees have been conferred upon him by four colleges: Oberlin, Hillsdale, Bucknell and Hobart. He is a member of Phi Beta Kappa; the Sons of the American Revolution; and the American Legion. He and his wife, Anne, make their home at 41 Park Avenue, and his office is at 521 Fifth Avenue, New York City.

DATE DUE